The Edupreneurs' Foundation

Principles of Educational Entrepreneurship

by
Luis R. Valentino, Ed.D.

Copyright © by Valgar, LLC. 2024

No part of this book may be reproduced in any form or by any electronic or mechanical means, including information storage and retrieval systems, without permission in writing from the author. The only exception is by a reviewer, who may quote short excerpts in a review.

For information, address Valgar, LLC, Indio, California 92201.

Although the author and publisher have made every effort to ensure that the information in this book was correct at press time, the author and publisher do not assume and hereby disclaim any liability to any party for any loss, damage, or disruption caused by errors or omissions, whether such errors or omissions result from negligence, accident, or any other cause.

This publication is designed to provide accurate and authoritative information with regard to the subject matter covered. It is sold with the understanding that the publisher does not render professional services. If legal advice or other expert assistance is required, the services of a competent professional should be sought. The fact that an organization or website is referred to in this work as a citation and/or a potential source of further information does not mean that the author or the publisher endorses the information the organization or website may provide or recommendations it may make. Please remember that Internet websites listed in this work may have changed or disappeared between its creation and its publication.

Valentino, Ed.D., Luis R.

The Edupreneurs' Foundation: Principles of Educational Entrepreneurship

ISBN-13: 978-0-9905660-3-8

1. education 2. entrepreneurship 3. Entrepreneurship

About the Author

Luis is an accomplished educator and transformational leader with over 35 years of experience in education. His career spans a range of roles in the education sector, including classroom teacher, site administrator, cabinet member, and superintendent. In these positions, he has led the development of organizational visions, sound education leadership, comprehensive learning experiences, and meaningful support systems to ensure those he serves have the tools they need to succeed.

He has applied his knowledge and skills in developing various edupreneurial ventures, including serving as CEO of Valgar, LLC. Through his ventures, he launched several resources, including the *District Leader* podcast, Wiredprofiles *Education Digest*, and Valgar Consulting.

Luis has been a college educator who taught at UCLA, USC, and Cal State, Los Angeles. He holds a BS degree from the University of Texas at Austin, an MS from Pepperdine University, an MA from Cal State, Los Angeles, and an Ed.D. from UCLA. He has also completed a post-doctoral program at Harvard University.

Luis is married to his wife, Elizabeth, and has two children, Audrey and Anthony.

Table of Contents

About the Author iv
Part I Edupreneurship 1
   Introduction: The Birth of Edupreneurship 2
   Chapter 1: Cultivating the Edupreneurial Mindset 8
   Chapter 2: Identifying Opportunities and Understanding Your Market 15
   Chapter 3: Developing and Testing Your Educational Product 22
   Chapter 4: Branding, Marketing, and Community Building 28
   Chapter 5: Technology Integration and Crafting Learning Experiences 37
   Chapter 6: The Business and Economics of Edupreneurship 43
   Chapter 7: Leadership, Team Building, and Operational Excellence 51
   Chapter 8: Navigating Legalities and Ethics 57
   Chapter 9: Measuring Impact and Scaling Your Venture 64
   Chapter 10: The Future of Edupreneurship and Personal Growth 70

Part 2 The Workbook 84
   Introduction 86
   Chapter 1: Cultivating the Edupreneurial Mindset 88
   Chapter 2: Identifying Opportunities and Understanding Your Market 96
   Chapter 3: Developing and Testing Your Educational Product 101
   Chapter 4: Branding, Marketing, and Community Building 108
   Chapter 5: Technology Integration and Crafting Learning Experiences 115
   Chapter 6: The Business and Economics of Edupreneurship 122
   Chapter 7: Leadership, Team Building, and Operational Excellence 129
   Chapter 8: Navigating Legalities and Ethics 137
   Chapter 9: Measuring Impact and Scaling Your Venture 142
   Chapter 10: The Future of Edupreneurship and Personal Growth 150
   Appendix A: Resources for Edupreneurs 157
   Appendix B: Glossary of Edupreneurship Terms 161
   Appendix C: Checklists and Templates for Start-Up Success 166

Part I
Edupreneurship

Introduction:
The Birth of Edupreneurship

In the nexus of education and entrepreneurship lies a brilliant gem known as edupreneurship—a fusion that ignites the transformative power of learning with the dynamism of business. At the heart of this movement is an alchemy that has begun to reshape how knowledge is delivered, consumed, and valued. As we unwrap the layers of edupreneurship's emergence, we come to understand its pivotal role in revolutionizing educational paradigms. Once just a mirror reflecting the status quo, education now stands poised at the cusp of innovation, with edupreneurs propelling an era where teaching transcends the bounds of traditional classrooms and learning becomes a lifelong journey of discovery. The history of edupreneurship, while embroidered with trials, is rich with triumphs that illustrate a clear trajectory: transformative change is not only possible but palpable. It's a landscape ripe with potential for those daring to leave indelible marks upon the canvas of education. Embracing edupreneurship doesn't just open doors—it creates new realms of possibility where the currency is creativity, the investment is intellect, and the returns are incalculable.

Overview of edupreneurship's emergence and its significance in transforming education

Edupreneurship has rapidly emerged as a revolutionary force, combining the dynamism of entrepreneurship with the noble mission of education. In this era of constant change and technological innovation, the traditional educational ecosystem is being challenged to evolve. It's here that edupreneurs have seized the opportunity, capitalizing on unmet needs and dissatisfactions within the system. These visionary individuals perceive gaps as potential niches for growth, building enterprises that not only address those gaps but also enhance learning outcomes and accessibility for all.

The significance of edupreneurship lies in its capacity to harness creativity and business acumen in service of educational advancement. Far from a mere commercial venture, these endeavors are fundamentally reshaping the landscape of learning. By prioritizing the learner's experience and employing cutting-edge pedagogical techniques, edupreneurs deliver personalized education tailored to the unique needs of each student. This responsiveness to the individual is pioneering a shift from the one-size-fits-all approach that has long been the hallmark of traditional education.

Moreover, edupreneurship embodies a spirit of relentless innovation. Where obstacles present themselves, edupreneurs envision solutions. Their ventures often introduce technologies and methodologies that may not have been previously considered within the confines of conventional schooling. Virtual reality, artificial intelligence, and adaptive learning platforms are a testament to the transformative power of edupreneurship, offering immersive and interactive educational experiences that were once the stuff of science fiction.

Edupreneurs also play a pivotal role in democratizing education, broadening access to those who might otherwise be excluded. Through online courses, digital tools, and mobile apps, education is no longer constrained by geography or socioeconomic status. This leveling of the playing field is perhaps one of the most profound ways in which edupreneurship is rewriting the script of education, offering hope and opportunity to countless aspiring learners around the globe.

The impact of edupreneurship transcends the immediate benefits of improved learning experiences. It cultivates an ecosystem of lifelong learners, individuals prepared to adapt and thrive amidst the rapid changes of the 21st century. In doing so, edupreneurs are not merely transforming education; they are preparing society for a future where learning never ends and opportunity abounds.

This book is designed to introduce and educate a diverse group of individuals involved in the education sector who are interested in entrepreneurship. The concept introduced is "edupreneurship," a blend of education and entrepreneurship. While the scope of this book can serve a broad audience, a focused audience may include:

- **Innovative Educators** are individuals who are always seeking new ways to engage their students or staff and believe in the power of innovation in education. They may be tech-savvy and active on social media. They may even participate in online forums and webinars to stay updated on the latest trends in education.

- **Education-focused Entrepreneurs** are individuals with a background in business who are interested in positively impacting the education sector. They are risk-takers and problem-solvers and are motivated by the potential of entrepreneurship to transform education.

- **School Administrators** are individuals who are interested in improving their school's learning environment and culture. They believe in collaborative learning and always seek effective strategies and resources to promote it.

- **EdTech Enthusiasts** are individuals with a passion for technology and education. They are excited about edtech startups and want to be part of this growing field.

- **Curriculum Developers** are individuals who work in school districts or companies. They understand curriculum materials and want to create engaging and effective learning materials. They may be tech-savvy, but more importantly, they are creative and believe in the power of curriculum resources to enhance learning.

These individuals are driven by a profound desire to enhance the educational landscape, fueled by their personal experiences and the challenges they've encountered in their careers. With a passion for innovation and a commitment to excellence, they are keen to explore edupreneurship, where they can apply their hard-earned insights to create meaningful solutions for fellow educators. They recognize the transformative potential of combining educational expertise with an entrepreneurial spirit and are eager to learn how to navigate this exciting intersection. Motivated by the possibility of effecting positive change, they are ready to embark on a journey to reshape education by becoming edupreneurs themselves.

The *Edupreneurs' Foundation: Principles of Educational Entrepreneurship* is crafted in two parts to guide aspiring edupreneurs from concept to execution. The first part delves into the rich history, foundational theories, and inspiring examples that underpin the edupreneurial landscape. The second part transitions into an interactive workbook format, inviting you to engage in reflection, design personalized strategies, and take actionable steps to kickstart your journey in the innovative world of educational entrepreneurship.

History of Edupreneurship As the learning landscape shifted beneath our feet, a new breed of innovators emerged, merging educators' zeal with entrepreneurs' acumen. This fusion of passion for education with the strategic savvy of business visionaries sparked what we now recognize as edupreneurship— a movement that has been quietly sculpting the future of educational engagement for decades.

The roots of this phenomenon didn't sprout overnight; tracing back through history, one can see that the groundwork for edupreneurship was laid as early as the age of correspondence courses and the advent of educational publications for the masses.

The zeitgeist of edupreneurship began to take a more defined shape with the rise of the internet. Access to knowledge became decentralized, opening avenues for savvy educators to reach a global audience. Early edupreneurs recognized the power of online platforms to break down the barriers of traditional classrooms, creating and selling courses that could be accessed from anywhere in the world. They showed us that education need not be confined to ivy-covered walls or state-funded curriculums; it could be nimble, diverse, and directly linked to the demands of the marketplace.

Through their innovative forays, edupreneurs started to disrupt the status quo. They sowed the seeds for a new kind of education— one that is tailored, tech-driven, and transcends geopolitical borders. They instituted models where learners could dictate their pace and path of learning. From subscription-based learning platforms to one-on-one tutoring businesses, these pioneers of edupreneurship have democratized knowledge and championed the cause of lifetime learning, a concept that echoes deeply in today's digital age.

The 21st century has seen the fruiting of this movement, with the emergence of massive open online courses (MOOCs), boot camps for coding, language learning apps, and personalized learning experiences. Edupreneurship has been about individual learning products and creating ecosystems that support learning, such as educational marketplaces and collaborative communities. Social impact has become intertwined with business models, empowering education innovators to address inequalities and contribute to societal upliftment through their ventures.

From its embryonic stages to today's dynamic environment, edupreneurship has evolved to encapsulate a spirit of educational innovation and a robust business strategy, offering significant value to learners and society. As you, the educator, administrator, or business leader, consider the landscape of edupreneurship, remember that its history is a testament to the transformative power of blending education with entrepreneurship. The trajectory of this movement inspires action and invites each one of us to step boldly into the role of educational change-maker, shaping not only the future of teaching and learning but also the fabric of our collective realities.

Chapter 1:
Cultivating the Edupreneurial Mindset

A vibrant landscape beckons those with a boundless and precise vision in the harmonious intersection where education meets entrepreneurship. These are the edupreneurs: innovators driven by the transformative power of learning, equipped with an entrepreneurial zeal to reimagine the dialogue of instruction. Cultivating an edupreneurial mindset is not just about the melding of two worlds but nurturing a particular way of being—a mix of foresight, adaptability, creativity, and an unyielding commitment to elevating educational experiences. Edupreneurship is defined as much by the mindset as by the action: to embody this philosophy is to see beyond traditional pedagogies and embrace the courage to disrupt, build, and continuously evolve. The characteristics of successful edupreneurs—a relentless pursuit of innovation and resilience in the face of challenges—are not innate traits but skills honed through mindful practice and reflection. As one embarks on this journey, the path may be fraught with challenges and setbacks. Yet, within these moments, the edupreneurial spirit is most profoundly tested and further fortified, laying the foundation for business ventures and the future of educational progress.

Defining Edupreneurship As we navigate through the versatile landscapes of education and entrepreneurship, it becomes imperative to pause and demarcate the contours of a term that lies at the epicenter of this transformative nexus - edupreneurship. What does it mean to be an edupreneur? At its core, edupreneurship fuses the passion for education with the innovative spirit of entrepreneurship. It's the pursuit of crafting educational opportunities that are instructive and inspiring, using the rigor of a business mindset to address educational needs and manifest change.

Edupreneurs are educators at heart, yet they also embody the tenacity and vision of entrepreneurs. They recognize that teaching and learning transcend the four walls of a traditional classroom. An edupreneur might develop cutting-edge curricula, launch educational technology startups, or establish tutoring services that disrupt conventional modes, all while aiming for sustainable growth and social impact. They're not confined to a single archetype; rather, they span a diverse spectrum - from teachers expanding their reach beyond their school districts to tech-savvy innovators designing apps that revolutionize how we learn.

However, edupreneurship isn't just about a good idea; it's about bringing that idea to fruition through strategic planning and execution. Edupreneurs are visionaries who identify gaps in the education market and fill them creatively while measuring the effectiveness of their solutions and ensuring they meet the highest pedagogical standards. They are trailblazers setting paths for learning that are adaptive, inclusive, and aligned with the evolving demands of society.

Moreover, the bedrock of edupreneurship lies in a commitment to value creation. This involves integrating ethical considerations into business models, ensuring equity in access to educational resources, and fostering a culture of continuous improvement. By sowing the seeds of entrepreneurship within the field of education, edupreneurs champion a cause that resonates with educators across the globe: a relentless drive to mold a brighter future through learning that informs and transforms.

Embracing edupreneurship requires juggling the pragmatism of running a business with the altruistic goal of educational advancement. It is that zealous intersection where profit and purpose collide, giving rise to innovative solutions that have the power to redraw the educational landscape. For those poised to embark on this journey, it's essential to understand this harmonious blend of educational mission with commercial strategy. It is the beating heart of edupreneurship – an enterprise that is as challenging as it is rewarding, as daring as it is definitive.

Characteristics of Successful Edupreneurs Unveiling the essential qualities that elevate an edupreneur above the crowd, this section delves deep into the heart of what it means to enter the educational sphere with a business mindset and thrive within it. The archetypal successful edupreneur exudes a harmonious blend of passion, perseverance, and acumen underpinned by an unwavering commitment to impact the realm of learning positively.

Foremost, passion fuels the edupreneur's journey like a ceaseless engine. This boundless energy for education ignites innovation, inspires others, and sets the visionary on a path that transcends monetary rewards. However, this passion must be yoked to a solid work ethic. The successful edupreneur knows that steadfast determination and tireless effort are the price of the ticket to the upper echelons of the market. They are characterized by their resilience in the face of setbacks, viewing obstacles as hidden opportunities to hone their craft and sharpen their strategy.

Next is adaptability—a characteristic that arms the edupreneur against the unpredictable tides of the educational and business landscapes. They are astute observers, making informed decisions backed by diligent research and data analysis. Yet, they remain agile, ready to pivot with the ever-changing demands of learners and the evolution of technology. This agility allows them to stay ahead of the curve, often pre-empting trends before they become mainstream, setting the pace rather than struggling to catch up.

Moreover, a successful edupreneur possesses an educator's soul and a businessperson's mind. Their approaches to scaling and monetization are as creative as their educational methods, blending sustainable business models with transformative educational practices. They balance profitability with purpose, ensuring their core mission—to educate—remains forefront while also achieving financial sustainability that allows their venture to grow and multiply its impact.

Lastly, successful edupreneurs are master communicators, adept at sharing their vision and rallying support from various stakeholders. They build communities, foster engagement, and craft narratives that resonate with their audience. Leadership exudes from their ability to inspire teams, students, and fellow educators, creating a ripple effect of enthusiasm and commitment. Through these communities, they establish a network of collaboration, learning, and support that upholds their enterprise and spreads its influence far and wide.

Cultivating an Innovative and Resilient Mindset is at the heart of thriving in the dynamic world of edupreneurship. It is a mindset that embraces the unknown, forges ahead through ambiguity, and sees challenges as opportunities for growth and innovation. To nurture this outlook, one must cultivate flexibility in thinking and an unwavering belief in one's ability to navigate and leverage change. For edupreneurs, setting sail on these uncharted waters means building a mentality that can adapt to rapid shifts and flourish amidst disruption.

The development of an innovative mindset begins with curiosity and a passion for learning. As educators and leaders, stepping outside of familiar boundaries is imperative. Encouraging experimentation and fostering a culture of inquiry within oneself sets the stage for breakthrough ideas and improvements. A resilient edupreneur actively seeks diverse perspectives, which can spark creativity and lead to unprecedented solutions. When obstacles arise, this individual sees them as essential learning curves, pivoting with agility and learning from every outcome.

Resilience, the other cornerstone of this mindset, is built on a foundation of tenacity and optimism. Understand that setbacks are not the end but rather signposts guiding you toward refinement and success. Maintaining an optimistic outlook enables one to continue journeying forward even after experiencing failure. Grit, the power to persevere with passion and determination, is what distinguishes those who achieve greatness from those who abandon the path too soon. The resilient edupreneur stands back up, questions what went awry, makes informed adjustments, and strides down the path once more with renewed vigor.

Creating a balance between innovation and resilience entails maintaining emotional intelligence and stress management. When the pressure mounts, a resilient edupreneur retains composure, keeping the end goal in view and managing stress through mindfulness and perspective. They understand that balance is not found in the absence of problems but in their graceful handling. Practicing mindfulness techniques can assist in becoming more responsive as opposed to reactive—a vital skill when leading a venture into the unknown territories of the education landscape.

Fostering this resilient and innovative mindset does not happen overnight; it is a cultivated skill. Like the most tenacious plants that thrive in rocky soils, it calls for constant nurturing, reflection, and an ever-growing toolbox of strategies. As an edupreneur, consider your mindset to be your most valuable asset. Invest time in adapting your thinking, take risks, celebrate every victory, no matter how small, and constantly seek feedback to fuel your progressive journey forward. This is how you'll anchor your vessel in the tumultuous seas of change and lead with passion and purpose.

Overcoming Common Challenges and Setbacks is a journey characteristic of every edupreneur's path to innovation and success. Within the fabric of education entrepreneurship lies myriad obstacles, each as a disguise for an invaluable lesson. The essence of edupreneurship doesn't lie in the absence of failure but rather in the tenacity and resilience to rise once we stumble.

When you're confronted with setbacks, it's crucial to first acknowledge the situation with a clear head. Emotional reactions might cloud judgment, so approach each challenge with a blend of pragmatism and optimism. Reflect and ask yourself: What can be learned from this experience? How can this inform your future decisions? Failure is often the best teacher, carving out the path for perseverance. Edupreneurs like you must harness such moments, refining your approach and adjusting their strategies. Document these learnings to avoid repeating the same mistakes and provide a roadmap for others in your team or network who can benefit from your experience.

It is also essential to keep a future-oriented mindset. Temporary setbacks should not derail long-term goals. Revisit your vision and the core values of your educational venture. Does your action align with your mission? If not, recalibrate. When faced with adversity, it's tempting to compromise or to veer off course. Instead, use this as an opportunity to strengthen your commitment to your edupreneurial mission. Additionally, infuse flexibility in your business models and teaching methodologies, making them adaptable and more resilient to change.

At every step, communication plays a pivotal role. Engage with your community of educators, students, and fellow edupreneurs. Reach out and share experiences to gain support and build a collective wealth of knowledge from which everyone can draw. The art of overcoming challenges is not a solo performance but a chorus, enriched by the voices of many. Let transparency and openness be your guiding principles, for within them lay the seeds of trust and collaboration, essential nutrients for any growing edupreneurial endeavor.

Last but certainly not least, pay heed to self-care. The journey of an edupreneur can be a taxing one, often requiring long hours and unswerving dedication. However, a clear mind and a healthy body are your greatest assets. Cultivate habits that ground you, keep stress in check, and rejuvenate your creative energies. Embrace continuous learning as an educational philosophy and a personal mantra. By committing to personal growth, you ensure that the edupreneur within is always equipped with the tools to navigate the unpredictable tides of the educational market.

Chapter 2: Identifying Opportunities and Understanding Your Market

There lies a fertile ground for innovation in the vibrant intersection where education meets entrepreneurship, but recognizing the right opportunities requires a discerning eye. With a cautious step forward from the foundational concepts of edupreneurship, this chapter serves as your map to navigate the educational landscape, unearthing hidden gems where your unique skills can make a significant impact. It's all about understanding the pulse of your market—identifying who your learners are, what they crave in their educational journey, and the unvoiced needs you can address. This chapter doesn't just scratch the surface; it delves deep into leveraging data as the compass to guide your entrepreneurial decisions, ushering you into territory ripe for exploration and ripe with possibility. As you traverse through these pages, remember that the market is dynamic, an ever-changing labyrinth of needs and preferences. But fear not, for within this complexity lies your chance to craft a venture that resonates, one that meets the learners where they are and elevates them to where they dream to be. Prepare to peel back the layers of the educational sector, uncovering new markets and cultivating an understanding so profound that it becomes the bedrock upon which you'll build your visionary educational solution.

Spotting Opportunities in the Education Landscape As we navigate the ever-evolving educational terrain, detecting and seizing opportunities becomes a pivotal skill. It must be honed with a strategic mindset and intuition born from an unwavering passion for education. This may involve identifying underserved niches, recognizing emerging trends that demand new learning solutions, or seeing how digital disruption can create openings for educational innovation. The astute edupreneur casts a wide net yet remains discerning enough to focus efforts where true impact can be made.

Understanding current educational challenges is key. When traditional systems falter or fail to address specific learner needs, gaps arise—these are your golden opportunities. It could be a lack of resources in rural areas, the need for bespoke learning materials for students with disabilities, or the absence of up-to-date career-oriented programs that align with the job market's demand. Since education's aim is to empower and enable, align your vision with these challenges. Develop solutions that bridge gaps, innovate pedagogy, or enhance access and quality for all learners.

Embrace the agility needed to navigate the education landscape by keeping a finger on the pulse of technology's role in learning. Consider the power of AI to personalize education or the potential of VR to transform history lessons into immersive experiences. Mobile learning, gamification, and online collaboration tools are not the future but the present. Pioneering edupreneurs will add value to the learning process by integrating these advancements in meaningful ways that resonate with students and educators alike.

Engage with the educational community to refine your opportunity-spotting acumen. This means participating in conversations, attending conferences, and joining professional groups. Within these spaces, listen more than you speak to understand the pain points of educators and learners. Act on insights gained from these interactions and translate them into actions and innovations that address real needs. In doing so, you'll mold opportunities and become a catalyst for change, illuminating paths for others to follow.

Last but not least, remember that spotting opportunities is not merely about the "what" but the "why". Align your entrepreneurial pursuits with the intrinsic values of education to enlighten, enrich, and elevate the human experience. Doing so ensures that your ventures maintain the heart of education, going beyond financial measures to create lasting, transformative impact in the lives of those you reach. In the vast landscape before you, let your compass be the betterment of learning and set sail towards horizons that beckon with the promise of what education might yet become.

The Customer: Understanding Your Learners

To truly engage in the art and science of edupreneurship, one must become laser-focused on the fundamental element of the educational endeavor: the learners. They are not mere customers but the very reason for the existence of an educational venture. Understanding who your learners are, what drives them, and their unique challenges represent more than just market research; it's a profound commitment to empathy and service. Whether your learners are school children, college students, professionals seeking skills enhancement, or lifelong learners branching into new disciplines, knowing their aspirations, learning styles, and motivational triggers is paramount.

When considering different learner segments, reflect on their diverse needs. What are their goals? How do they prefer to access information? Some may thrive in a community-driven environment, while others seek self-paced, autonomous learning experiences. Acknowledge that demographics such as age, location, and educational background will also shape their expectations and how they interact with your content. By capturing this mosaic of learner profiles, you tailor your educational solutions, designing learning experiences that resonate deeply and yield transformative outcomes.

Data and observations become the compass for navigating the learning landscape of your audience. Engage in an active dialogue with potential learners through surveys, interviews, or informal conversations. This direct feedback loop helps sculpt a detailed understanding of the learner's journey—highlighting pain points, uncovering aspirations, and tracking the moments of frustration and exhilaration. Edupreneurs harmonize this insight with their vision, creating a synergy that elevates educational offerings from mere products to catalysts for personal and professional growth.

Yet, remember, as you cultivate this understanding, you are not just a silent observer but a contributor to the educational narrative. Your actions and choices shape the learning environment, constructing a space that invites exploration and curiosity. This means being adaptive and responsive, ready to evolve your approach as you gain further insight into your learners' evolving needs. Flexibility ensures that your educational venture remains relevant, impactful, and deeply rooted in the genuine aspirations of those you serve.

Ultimately, understanding your learners is an ongoing pursuit, akin to nurturing a garden. It demands patience, attention, and a willingness to grow alongside your learners. Just as the best teachers adapt to the needs of their students, the successful edupreneur aligns their educational offerings with the nuanced dynamics of their audience. In doing so, you craft learning experiences that inform, inspire, empower, and act as a bridge to new horizons for each individual who embarks on the journey with you.

Using Data to Drive Decision-Making As the landscape of education shifts beneath our feet, we take an intelligent leap into the epicenter of change. In embracing edupreneurship, the astute harnessing of data is not just a recommendation but a cornerstone of success. Making informed decisions pivots on understanding your market, and this is where data transforms into your most trusted advisor. It guides your vision, ensuring you make evidence-based choices that align with the needs and desires of your audience.

Data is the compass that points toward opportunities yet unseen. It tells a story of the learner's journey, shines light on their challenges, and unveils their achieving moments. Educators and edupreneurs should lean into this narrative, gathering quantitative and qualitative insights to tailor their offerings. Whether through surveys, learning analytics, or market research, your goal is to decode these data points into actionable strategies that resonate with your learners and differentiate you in the marketplace. The thoughtful analysis of data shapes an adaptive framework for innovation that responds nimbly to an ever-evolving educational terrain.

Yet, the mere collection of data is not a panacea. Education ignites the core of human potential, and with that understanding comes a responsibility. Interpret carefully, be judicious in your inferences, and prioritize the security and privacy of those you serve. It is a delicate balance—maximizing the utility of information with the ethical considerations it demands. This stewardship of data is a testament to the trust your learners place in you, and honoring that is paramount in forging lasting connections.

Fused with the principles of edupreneurship, data-driven decision-making becomes a catalyst for educational transformation. It sharpens your focus on what truly matters: delivering value at the confluence of learning, innovation, and entrepreneurship. Your mission is to not only educate but also inspire and empower. In this charged space, let data illuminate the path to fulfilling the aspirations of every learner, thereby carving your unique imprint in the educational cosmos.

Melding data into your decision-making process also prepares you for the future—an age where your adaptability will be continuously tested. The role of the edupreneur is dynamic, and you must be poised to pivot with the agility of thought. Grounded in robust data analysis, your ventures will more adeptly weather shifting educational paradigms and foster success. Cultivate this critical competency, and watch as it transforms your venture and the very face of education itself.

Exploring New Markets and Opportunities

In the evolving education landscape, harnessing the potential of untouched markets and fresh opportunities is vital for the flourishing edupreneur. The skill lies in navigating beyond conventional boundaries, discerning gaps in educational services, and creating value where it was not previously perceived. Whether your aspiration lies in revolutionizing kindergarten readiness programs or transforming continuing education for seniors, remember: every demographic holds the promise of uncharted territory.

Understanding your market does not mean confining your vision to the obvious and the already-served. A vast expanse of learning needs is waiting to be addressed across different cultures, professions, and communities. Consider a database architect in Buenos Aires who yearns to learn Eastern philosophy or a stay-at-home parent in Nebraska looking to pivot into a graphic design career. Strive to empathize deeply with the unique educational hurdles such diverse groups face. By casting a wide, yet thoughtful and informed net, you're poised to unveil niches ripe with possibility for innovative educational solutions.

When contemplating expansion into new markets, don't shy away from leveraging technology as a bridge to reach these previously inaccessible audiences. Utilizing online platforms and digital tools enables you to transcend geographical limitations, creating a learning environment as boundless as your ambition. Initiate dialogues, gather feedback, and begin to tailor educational experiences that resonate on a personal level with your newfound learners; somewhere in this interactive crucible, the seeds of opportunity germinate.

It's equally crucial to consider collaborations and partnerships that might unlock doors to novel markets. Linking arms with local leaders, businesses, and cultural organizations can position you at the epicenter of needs you aspire to meet. Through such synergies, your edupreneurial venture gains both relevance and reach, fostering a web of connections that solidify your standing as an educator and an innovator.

In conclusion, charting a course into the unknown may be daunting, but it is a voyage filled with the promise of growth and the thrill of discovery. As you stand poised to set sail, let your vision for education be your compass and anchor. New markets and opportunities await — it's time to raise your sails and capture the winds of change.

Chapter 3:
Developing and Testing Your Educational Product

In the noble quest to shape the future through education, crafting an educational product is the cornerstone of your edupreneurial journey. Imagine the alchemy of merging creativity with analytical rigor; this is where your vision starts to breathe life, meticulously transforming into a tangible offering that carries the potential to revolutionize learning outcomes. Take the first step by envisioning a curriculum or tool that captivates the imagination and stays true to pedagogical soundness. Blend the art of storytelling with evidence-based results to encapsulate the essence of your teachings. With your draft in hand, embark on the gratifying process of sculpting your content—a process reminiscent of a gardener pruning, refining until what remains is nothing short of splendid.

The mantra "test, iterate, enhance" should resonate with your inner edupreneurial spirit. Introduce your brainchild to a small segment of your audience, and observe. Dive into the feedback loop, where each critique is a golden nugget of insight, propelling your product closer to perfection. This iterative cycle, although at times painstaking, is quintessential in forging an outcome that doesn't just meet expectations but exceeds them. As you refine your product, remember that an educational tool is only as effective as the learning it fosters. Therefore, measure, adjust, and stay attuned to the ever-changing landscape of educational needs. Your final offering will not merely be an artifact of knowledge but an instrument of inspiration, igniting a relentless curiosity that echoes through the corridors of learning for years to come.

Designing Compelling Content and Ensuring Educational Efficacy lies at the heart of any educational venture. When creating content, an edupreneur must ignite a sense of wonder and engagement that transforms passive listeners into active participants. Start with the learner's needs and goals. What makes their heart beat faster? What quandaries keep them up at night? Use these insights as your guide to crafting content that not only captivates but also meets a clear educational objective. A rule of thumb is to always question how each piece of content serves the learner's journey toward mastery.

However, designing content that sparkles with intrigue is but a fragment of the quest. To ensure educational efficacy, one must validate that content leads to genuine learning outcomes. This is achieved through deliberate scaffolding—constructing a learning pathway that methodically builds on prior knowledge. Think of it as creating a cognitive roadmap that shows the destination and every key checkpoint along the way. Ensure each segment of your content serves as a milestone, marking progress and deepening understanding.

Alignment with educational standards cannot be overstated. But go beyond ticking boxes. Infuse your content with real-world applications to make learning relevant. Learners crave practicality—a chance to apply what they've absorbed in authentic scenarios. Whether through simulations, case studies, or hands-on projects, relevancy enriches learning and embeds knowledge. Furthermore, integrate assessment as a seamless part of the learning process. Formative assessments provide ongoing checkpoints that offer timely feedback to both the learner and the educator, fine-tuning the learning experience to personal needs and pacing.

Personalization is a powerful tool in modern edupreneurship. Each learner journeys at their own pace, with unique strengths and challenges. A one-size-fits-all approach is a relic of the past. Develop your content to adapt to meet each learner where they are. Use data and feedback to create differentiated paths within your content, allowing learners to explore avenues tailored to their individual profiles. This is where iterative design comes into play. Test and refine your offerings based on actual user experience to create a dynamic learning environment that evolves with its users.

Ultimately, your educational content's potency is measured by how it impacts learners. It's about the 'ah-ha' moments that happen when concepts click and new perspectives are shaped through application and reflection. Keep your pulse on these outcomes and let them guide your design process. Empower your learners to consume knowledge and grow from it—turning information into insight and insight into action. As an edupreneur, you're not just disseminating knowledge but crafting experiences that form the foundation for lifelong learning and transformation.

Lean Edupreneurship: Testing and Iterating compels one to adopt a mindset agile and adaptive, functioning much like the skillful educator who tailors lesson plans responsive to fluctuating classroom dynamics. In this sphere of edupreneurship, you become a lifelong learner, where your product—or educational service—is the subject of ongoing experimentation and refinement. This approach draws on the principles of the lean startup methodology, which is not limited to the business world but is extraordinarily fitting for educational ventures. Here, the focus turns to creating simple versions of your offering, collecting user feedback, and iterating quickly, avoiding over-investment in unproven ideas.

Picture the development of an educational tool, possibly a new app that aims to simplify complex mathematical concepts for high school students. The lean method does not have you develop a feature-complete product before its first test run. Instead, it urges you to craft a Minimum Viable Product (MVP)—a functional yet barebones version whose core aim is to begin the learning process as swiftly as possible. Once in the hands of actual users, valuable insights emerge from real-world interaction, informing the direction of your next iteration with much greater precision than speculation ever could.

Dive into this testing phase with an eye for qualitative and quantitative feedback. Surveys, interviews, and direct observations transform into the compass that guides your entrepreneurial journey. And yet, this is not to suggest that every piece of feedback should reroute your path; the art lies in discerning patterns, identifying what aligns with your educational mission, and recognizing that each iteration cycles closer to a truly resonant product. With this actionable data, you refine your offering, adjust features, and remedy challenges, all while remaining nimble in anticipation of the next cycle of feedback and improvements.

It's essential, however, not to confound iterating with aimless wandering. Your vision should remain steadfast, guiding the iterative process toward a well-defined end goal. Each loop through the cycle is a step forward, a hypothesis tested, a question answered, and a lesson learned. Remember, your venture's success lies in its ability to foster learning and growth—not just in your users but within your own entrepreneurial practices as well. As you iterate, keep your eyes open for unforeseen opportunities, ready to harness their potential.

Edupreneurs, as agents of change in the educational landscape, must always stay malleable, eager to adapt and improve their offerings. Embrace the discomfort of uncertainty—after all, it is the fertile ground from which innovation sprouts. Trust in the process of testing and iterating, for it is through this relentless pursuit of excellence and relevance that your educational product will truly flourish and make its most significant impact on the world of learning.

Creating Minimum Viable Products (MVPs) In the journey of transforming an educational innovation from concept to classroom, creating a Minimum Viable Product, or MVP, is a pivotal step. The essence of an MVP is grounded in its simplicity; it's a version of your product that allows you to collect the maximum amount of validated learning about customers with the least effort. This approach enables you to test your assumptions, refine your vision, and deliver an educational tool that genuinely meets the needs of your learners without investing exorbitant time and resources upfront.

An MVP is centered around the core functionality that solves the initial problem or fulfills your identified basic needs. For edupreneurs, this often translates to a scaled-down yet functional educational product that can be offered to a small group of users or a pilot classroom. You must resist the temptation to create a feature-rich first version; here, less is indeed more. Focusing on the core value proposition and delivering it effectively provides a platform for genuine feedback, fostering an environment where successes and failures serve as crucial learning opportunities.

Feedback from your MVP is invaluable. As users interact with your educational product, observe their behavior, gather their insights, and ask poignant questions. Are they engaged? What learning outcomes are achieved? How could the product better serve both educators and learners? This information will be the guiding light to iterate and improve your offering. Remember that in the realm of edupreneurship, your first idea is rarely your final product, and adaptability is a hallmark of success.

While crafting your MVP, consider the balance between educational efficacy and technological feasibility. Your product should resonate with your target audience and integrate seamlessly into the existing educational infrastructure. Take calculated risks, but ensure that your product remains practical and accessible. In this nascent stage, the feedback loop is your greatest ally, and refinement is a continual process driven by real-world applications and results-driven improvements.

To edupreneurs poised at the brink of creating and launching MVPs, view this phase as an exhilarating opportunity to witness your vision take shape. The development of an MVP is not just about building an educational tool; it's about igniting a conversation with your audience and laying a strong foundation for future growth. As you navigate this journey, remain steadfast in your commitment to education, innovation, and the transformative potential of your venture. Creating an MVP is not merely the first step in product development; it's a bold stride toward meaningful change in the world of education.

Chapter 4:
Branding, Marketing, and Community Building

Transitioning from the initial stages of product development, Chapter 4 delves into the quintessential elements of Branding, Marketing, and Community Building. This is where the heart of your edupreneurial venture beats loudest, as your brand's identity becomes your flag planted in the fertile soil of educational innovation. Crafting a brand that resonates with your core values isn't just about logos or taglines; it's about weaving the story of your mission into every strand of your business's fabric. Marketing becomes an extension of that story, a bridge connecting your powerful narrative to the lives of educators, students, and lifelong learners seeking transformation through education. Authenticity in this endeavor isn't just recommended. It's imperative for it's the genuine desire to enrich minds that ignites community engagement and fosters social responsibility. Leveraging social media and strategic networking amplifies your message and ushers in a wave of collaborative opportunities, inviting a constant exchange of insights that further strengthens the community you've set out to build. A responsive community thrives on involvement and shared values. As you inspire and are inspired by this ever-expanding network, you harness a collective power that propels both your mission and your market presence forward, creating a learning ecosystem that's vibrant, inclusive, and poised for sustained growth.

Building Your Educational Brand As you navigate through the chapters of turning vision into reality, the significance of brand identity cannot be overstated. In the world of edupreneurship, your brand epitomizes your promise to your learners, your educational philosophy, and the unique value you offer. It's the story that bridges you and your audience – a narrative that resonates with the minds and hearts of those you seek to educate, inspire, and engage.

Your brand should be a reflection of your core mission and values, allowing you to carve out a distinctive niche in the educational landscape. It starts by understanding what sets you apart. What key insights or innovative methods are you bringing to the table? How does your experience or approach translate into a benefit for your learners? Solidifying your unique selling proposition is the cornerstone of your branding strategy, and it must be communicated consistently across all platforms and mediums.

Visual identity is a pivotal element in building your educational brand. Consider your logo, color palette, and typography. These should align with the overall tone and message of your brand, which should be tailored to speak to your target demographic in a compelling and approachable way. Consistency is vital – from the design of your website and promotional materials to the delivery of your courses and presentations. This visual harmony creates recognition and trust, instilling confidence in potential learners and stakeholders that you're the go-to source for educational innovation and value.

Constructing a strong narrative lays a firm foundation for your brand. It's about creating an emotional connection with your audience by sharing your journey, overcoming challenges, successes, and the transformative power of education you've witnessed or facilitated. Telling this story isn't just beneficial for marketing; it allows for a deeper engagement with your community, fostering loyalty and advocacy among those who believe in your mission. Your story isn't a static piece; it evolves and grows as you do, becoming richer and more intricate with every student you help and every goal you accomplish.

Lastly, it's imperative to live your brand. Authenticity can't be faked. It's demonstrated through your interactions, content, responsiveness, and dedication to your educational goals. Engage with your community, gather feedback, and show that you talk and walk the walk. This sincerity will earn respect and elevate your brand above the noise of competition, securing your position as a trusted, inspirational landmark in the edupreneurial ecosystem. Your educational brand is more than a logo or a tagline; it's an experience – an ongoing, dynamic encounter that has the power to change lives, including your own.

Marketing with Authenticity begins with the understanding that your mission extends beyond economic gains; it's about creating genuine value and demonstrating an unwavering commitment to your audience's growth and transformation. In the cosmos of an edupreneurial venture, such authenticity isn't just valuable; it's essential. It allows you to present your educational products not as mere commodities but as keystones in an individual's journey to enlightenment and empowerment.

In this landscape, trust is your most precious asset. To cultivate trust, you must mirror the clarity and truth you wish to see in your learners. Your marketing messages should stem from your authentic experiences and the core benefits your educational offerings aim to provide. Remember, your audience—educators, administrators, or lifelong learners—is astutely perceptive of disingenuity. They search for solutions that resonate with their aspirations and challenges and connect most profoundly with voices that speak not just to their intellect but to their hearts as well.

Storytelling is the golden thread in the tapestry of authentic marketing. Your narrative should weave together the threads of your passion for education, the transformative power of your product, and the success stories of those who have benefitted from it. When your marketing reflects your educational journey and impact on others, you align yourself with the communities you serve. This alignment forges strong connections and catalyzes organic advocacy as satisfied learners share their experiences with others.

The resonance of authenticity extends into how you interact with your market. Communicate with transparency and vulnerability; acknowledging the iterative nature of educational innovations can engender great respect and loyalty. Although perfection is unattainable, pursuing excellence with humility can inspire your audience. Encourage dialogue, invite feedback, and show that you are not only an educator but also a dedicated learner, constantly evolving your offerings in response to the needs and insights of your community.

Ultimately, edupreneurs who thrive are those who approach marketing as an extension of their teaching—endeavoring to enlighten, engage, and encourage their audience. Your edupreneurial brand, when steeped in authenticity, attracts not just customers but disciples of your philosophy, supporters of your mission, and contributors to your vision of transforming education. Thus, market with a heart of service, and every educational tool you create becomes more than a product—it becomes a beacon of progress and a testament to the boundless potential of every learner it touches.

Community Engagement and Social Responsibility As edupreneurs, we carry forward a crucial mantle of responsibility that extends beyond the confines of our ventures. It is our duty to immerse ourselves in the fabric of communities, recognizing the intricate patterns that connect education with societal progression. The essence of community engagement is not merely to market products or disseminate information but rather to listen, learn, and ignite transformative dialogues that resonate with the core of local concerns and ambitions.

Imagine a scenario where your educational initiative becomes the bridge that links learning with real-world impact, inspiring learners to become active citizens and stewards of change. By fostering partnerships with local businesses, non-profits, and civic groups, edupreneurs can create synergistic relationships that amplify their message while contributing to the community's well-being. In the classroom of life, every edupreneur should strive to be the benevolent facilitator who helps each member find their voice and leverage it for the collective good.

Embrace social responsibility as a pillar of your edupreneurial model. This means addressing educational gaps, being environmentally conscious, advocating for equity and inclusion, and leading by example in ethical practices. When we conscientiously align our businesses with these principles, we ascend beyond the role of service providers—we become catalysts for a hopeful, more enlightened future. Your educational offerings should ideally embody the virtues of sustainability and foster an ethos of global citizenship among learners.

To a novice in the world of edupreneurship, community engagement might seem like navigating uncharted waters. Yet, the successful edupreneur knows that the compass that leads to profound impact lies within the heart of the community itself. Through volunteer initiatives, scholarship programs, and participatory workshops, we further ingrain our roots into the soil of mutual trust and respect. These engagements act as conduits for resource exchange, knowledge sharing, and, most importantly, for cementing lasting relationships that go beyond transactional interactions.

In conclusion, community engagement and social responsibility should not be treated as afterthoughts in the edupreneurial journey; they are, in fact, foundational. As pioneers of educational innovation, we must harness the collective spirit, encouraging all stakeholders to join hands toward a future where learning and humane values coalesce. Through our endeavors, we possess the power to shape minds, touch hearts, and leave an indelible imprint on society—one that will inspire others to perpetuate this cycle of positive change and progress.

Effective Use of Social Media and Networking The landscape of education is continually evolving, and as we venture further into a world where knowledge and networking are currency, your prowess with social media becomes a critical tool. The art of social media engagement isn't just about posting—it's about building relationships, establishing thought leadership, and creating communities that resonate with your brand's ethos and educational goals.

Imagine each social platform as a vibrant classroom. It's a space where conversations are sparking, ideas are exchanged, and inspiration strikes. The tech-savvy teacher doesn't stand at the head of this classroom, talking at students; instead, they weave through the desks, engaging and empowering their learners with every interaction.

To capitalize on these spaces, it's essential to identify the platforms where your audience congregates. Are they thumbing through tweets, double-tapping on Instagram, or networking on LinkedIn? Once you find your arena, it's about curating a presence that speaks with clarity and passion about the educational solutions you offer.

Content is the linchpin of your social media strategy. It's more than just attractive visuals; it's about storytelling that captivates. Think of your content as the lesson plan and every post as an integral part of the curriculum. Each piece should educate, inform, or enlighten your followers, providing value at every step of their journey with your brand.

Engagement is not a one-way street. Like best educators foster open dialogue with their students, your response and interaction with followers determine how your community grows. Responding to comments, addressing concerns, and celebrating successes alongside your audience makes your brand approachable and trustworthy.

Networking expands beyond simple connections—it's about fostering meaningful relationships. Whether it's with fellow educators, influencers, or potential partners, each interaction should be as genuine and intentional as those you aim to create with your learners. These connections can often become instrumental in cross-promotion and collaborative efforts that amplify your reach.

Consistency in your messaging and posts is key. Just as in teaching, where routine and structure support a learning environment, regularly scheduled content maintains your audience's attention. It builds anticipation, sets expectations, and establishes a rhythm for your online presence.

Metrics are your grade book. Monitor what resonates with your audience through likes, shares, and comments. Use analytics tools to understand how your content performs, and let these insights guide your strategy. It's essential for you to know what is captivating for your audience to refine your approach and make data-driven decisions continually.

Authenticity should shine through your social media presence. In education, nothing is more valued than genuine engagement and belief in one's mission. Let your unique personality and passion for education be evident in every post, every campaign, and every interaction. Your authenticity paves the way for connections that transcend the digital realm.

Storytelling is as old as time, yet it remains a powerful tool. Through the narratives you share, you educate and engage simultaneously. The tales of success, struggle, and the journey of growth resonate deeply, allowing your audience to see the human side of your edupreneurial venture and identify with your mission personally.

User-generated content is like homework you didn't have to assign. Encourage your followers to share their stories and experiences with your educational products or services. It provides authentic endorsements for your brand and fosters a sense of belonging and community amongst your audience.

While hashtags may seem trivial, they serve a purpose akin to keywords in an academic paper. They improve visibility, create conversation threads, and connect you with larger movements or discussions relevant to education. Use them effectively to join bigger conversations or to create your own.

Collaborations with influencers and thought leaders can catapult your visibility. Seek relationships with notable figures in your field who embody the values and mission of your venture. Just like a guest speaker in a classroom, they can bring new perspectives and audiences to your brand.

Live sessions and webinars are the digital equivalent of office hours or guest lectures. They provide real-time engagement opportunities and can help deepen the relationship you have with your audience. This face-to-face interaction, even through a screen, enhances trust and allows immediate feedback and collaboration.

Investing in paid advertising must be done with the same discernment as an educational resource. It's crucial to target the right demographics and craft compelling messages that align with your branding. Paired with organic growth strategies, paid campaigns can effectively boost your reach and impact.

Finally, don't underestimate the power of a call to action. Just as you would guide your students towards a goal in their learning, direct your followers towards taking the next step with your brand, be it signing up for a course, engaging with a post, or sharing their experiences. Guide them with clarity and purpose; they'll be your collaborators in education and growth.

Mapping social media strategies into pedagogical approaches enriches your connection with your audience. Remember, at its core, social media is about fostering a community of engaged learners and influencers. Use it wisely for opportunities to ignite discussions, influence opinions, and pioneer educational transformations that lie within its realms.

Chapter 5:
Technology Integration and Crafting Learning Experiences

As we venture further into the realm of edupreneurship, embracing the digital revolution becomes imperative. Chapter 5 delves into the seamless integration of technology and the art of creating transformative learning experiences. In a world where knowledge is abundant, and attention is scarce, the savvy edupreneur harnesses the latest educational tools to captivate minds and foster deep, engaging learning. But it's not merely about using technology for its sake – it's about choosing the right tools to complement educational goals, amplify student engagement, and enhance understanding. By effectively blending technology with pedagogy, edupreneurs craft learning paths that are rich in content and empathetic to the learner's journey, facilitating a blend of synchronous and asynchronous learning tailored to individual needs. This chapter guides you through the intricate dance of technology and education, ensuring that each step is purposeful, each click reveals a new horizon, and every screen time becomes a gateway to learning that resonates and endures.

Leveraging Technology and Tools

In the journey to carve out a unique space in the educational landscape, embracing cutting-edge technology and tools stands as a cornerstone for edupreneurs. The fusion of technology in education enhances learning experiences and amplifies educational products' reach and efficacy. To navigate this terrain, one must be discerning with the myriad of tools available, aligning each selection with learners' vision, objectives, and needs. As we delve deeper into the digital age, your role as an edupreneur necessitates fluency in digital tools, from content creation platforms to learning management systems and analytics software.

Content is king, but delivery is its crown. Implementing intuitive and collaborative platforms encourages engagement and fosters an interactive community of learners. Video conferencing software, online forums, and virtual whiteboards transcend geographical boundaries, knitting together a global classroom. Use these platforms to your advantage, ensuring dynamic interaction and seamless communication. Analytics and data-tracking tools, on the other hand, serve as your compass, guiding decisions and refining strategies based on actual user engagement and learning outcomes. With insights gleaned from data, you can tailor experiences that resonate with your audience, fostering personalized and adaptive learning pathways.

Yet, technology is not solely a means to deliver content; it is equally important as a marketing and networking lever. Social media tools and online advertising platforms offer potent means to amplify your brand's voice and to connect with your community. Craft content that engages educates, and excites. Leverage Search Engine Optimization (SEO) to ensure your offerings rise to the surface in a sea of digital content. When used with intention and savvy, these digital tools expand your reach and fortify the bonds with your growing audience.

As boundaries blur between education and technology, the rise of AI and machine learning promises unprecedented capabilities in personalized learning, providing an opportunity for edupreneurs to design sophisticated, adaptive learning experiences. While the detailed exploration of AI's role is unpacked elsewhere in this book, it's crucial to understand its potential for creating scalable, individualized educational paths – demystifying complex concepts and offering real-time, data-driven support to each learner.

Despite the allure of these sophisticated tools, remember that at the heart of edupreneurship is the craft of creating meaningful learning experiences. Technologies are your allies, not your endgame. They are the vessels through which your innovative educational visions come to life and reach the hands, hearts, and minds of learners worldwide. Choose tools that enhance rather than complicate, and always keep the learning journey at the forefront of your edupreneurial mission. In this techno-centric era, the tech-savvy edupreneur melds the best of both worlds, pairing the touch of a teacher's human insight with the leverage of digital omnipresence, sculpting a legacy that transcends traditional classrooms and redefines education for future generations.

Crafting Impactful Learning Experiences As an edupreneur, your quest is to create educational paradigms that convey knowledge and truly enliven it. The alchemy of impactful learning experiences lies in the delicate balance of content, context, and connection. To weave education that resonates deeply with your learners, it is vital to architect journeys that are not merely informational but transformational. Learning experiences rooted in relevance and engagement can ignite intellectual curiosity and establish a foundation for lifelong learning. It's about crafting a narrative around the content, empowering learners to explore and make meaning for themselves.

One must blend didactic precision with narrative allure in designing potent learning modules. Edupreneurs often stand at the forefront of pedagogical innovation, harnessing interactive storytelling, problem-based learning, and experiential activities. Each module and each lesson should dance to the tune of active learning—where learners do not passively absorb but actively participate. Engage your audience through case studies relevant to real-world scenarios, simulations that demand critical thinking, and discussions that kindle meaningful dialogue. Educational experiences of this caliber invite learners to apply, synthesize, and evaluate information in ways that traditional lectures simply can't match.

Accessibility and inclusivity should hallmark your offerings. Learning experiences are most impactful when they are designed with a keen understanding of diverse learning styles and needs. A multifaceted approach, encompassing various formats like videos, texts, infographics, and interactive modules, can cater to this diversity, ensuring no learner is left behind. Furthermore, integrating assessments and feedback systems that are constructive and continuous can significantly amplify the learning outcomes. It isn't merely about testing knowledge but about fostering improvement and celebrating growth through personalized insights that encourage learners to reach their full potential.

Technology holds the power to transform and scale learning experiences in unprecedented ways. Embrace the digital tools and platforms that elevate convenience and adaptability—essential components in today's fast-paced world. However, beware of the trap of using technology for technology's sake. Every digital tool you integrate should have a definitive pedagogical purpose, enhancing the learning journey rather than complicating it. The judicious use of technology can expand boundaries, connect learners globally, and equip them with the skills they need in a digitally driven society.

Finally, in your edupreneurial endeavor, remember that emotion and learning are intrinsically linked. When learners feel, they remember. Foster an environment rich with emotional resonance—where triumphs are celebrated, challenges are embraced with a growth mindset, and the value of perseverance is instilled. The most impactful learning experiences are those that inspire change, not just in thought but in behavior and action. Your role is not only to inform but to inspire, not only to teach but to transform. Through the mindful crafting of experiences that touch the heart and challenge the mind, you are sculpting the future of education and the potential of every learner who crosses your path.

The Role of AI and Machine Learning in Education As we venture deeper into the heart of educational innovation, it becomes clear that artificial intelligence (AI) and machine learning are revolutionizing the landscape. Integrating these technologies in education is not just a fleeting trend but a powerful tool reshaping how educators approach teaching and learners engage with knowledge. The intuitive capabilities of AI and the predictive nature of machine learning algorithms can elevate the educational experience, providing personalized learning journeys for every student and creating a collaborative environment where humans and machines work side by side for optimal learning outcomes.

AI can automate administrative tasks in the classroom, freeing educators to focus on what they do best—guide, mentor, and inspire. For edupreneurs, this means that their ventures can be more efficient, impactful, and scalable. Machine learning algorithms analyze data to draw insights into learning patterns, helping educators tailor the educational content to the unique needs of their students. This adaptive learning technology ensures that each learner is engaged at just the right level of challenge, crucially considering their individual learning style, pace, and preferences.

Moreover, AI-driven analytics can identify trends and predict which educational products or services will be most effective, thereby informing ecopreneurs' strategic decisions. These insights are invaluable, as they enable a proactive approach to refining educational offerings, ensuring that your endeavor stays ahead of the curve. Machine learning is not about replacing the educator but rather augmenting their capabilities, creating an environment where personalized education is not a luxury but a standard.

As edupreneurs, embracing AI and machine learning is tantamount to planting a tree under whose shade future generations will learn. These tools are not just about optimizing current educational practices but also about laying the groundwork for new, innovative approaches to learning that we have yet to imagine. They can break down barriers to education, ensuring accessibility and inclusivity, ultimately democratizing learning across the globe. This intersection of technology and education holds untapped potential, waiting for visionary edupreneurs to harness, refine, and direct it toward transformative educational experiences.

Imagine a world where education is dynamic, interactive, and continuously evolving—a world where AI and machine learning catalyze lifelong learning and foster an insatiable curiosity. As edupreneurs, it's within your power to create this reality. By integrating AI and machine learning into your educational ventures, you're not only shaping the future of education but also participating in a broader dialogue about the kind of future we want to create—one where each learner's potential can be fully realized with the help of intelligent, data-driven technologies.

Chapter 6:
The Business and Economics of Edupreneurship

Embarking on the path of edupreneurship is more than a pedagogical pursuit; it's a journey through the vibrant intersection of education and business. Substantial knowledge of economics is vital for sustaining the theater of innovation that edupreneurship brings to learning. Within this chapter, let's demystify the art of revenue generation in education, unraveling the various monetization strategies that transform skills and knowledge into sustainable income streams. A keen eye for financial planning is not just recommended; it's essential, and when we think of budgeting and financial oversight, it's not about curtailing creative flow—it's about fueling growth and scalability. Furthermore, securing funding through angel investors, grants, or crowdsourcing is an adventure requiring both strategic acumen and an unflagging spirit. The essence of this chapter lies in empowering you, the edupreneur, with the financial confidence to weave educational missions with economic vigor, ensuring your entrepreneurial tapestry is rich in content, value, and impact.

Understanding Education Economics As we approach this pivotal topic within the intricate tapestry of edupreneurship, it's imperative to grasp the essence of economics in the realm of education. Within the structured classrooms and whiteboards lies an ecosystem thriving with potential, a landscape where value creation meets the demand for knowledge and skill development. This intersection spotlights the economic principles that underlie successful educational ventures. Considering the economic facets of edupreneurship is not merely about profit margins or fiscal prudence; it is also about understanding the value exchange between educator and learner and how that translates into sustainable business models.

A comprehensible approach to education economics enables edupreneurs to align market needs with educational services, starting with the core principle of supply and demand. Educators are uniquely positioned to supply transformative learning experiences for today's dynamic market. In doing so, they must identify who requires these experiences, the value these learners place on them, and how they are willing to engage. These parameters help shape an edupreneur's offerings through standard curriculums, online modules, workshops, or various other educational formats.

But how does one ascertain the true economic value of an educational offering? This begins with a thorough analysis of costs—from content creation and delivery to marketing and customer service—and the role of pricing strategies to balance affordability with the need to support a financially healthy enterprise. A deep dive into unit economics will reveal how each educational product contributes to or detracts from the overall financial well-being of the venture. The astute edupreneur taps into pricing models, bundling strategies, and value perception to captivate and retain learners, thereby ensuring a harmonious flow between educational impact and economic viability.

Moreover, education economics involves studying and applying financial acumen to nurture a thriving business in the competitive landscape of lifelong learning. The key lies in creating outstanding educational content and orchestrating resources effectively to achieve operational efficiency. Investment in technology, talent hiring, and customer base expansion should be well-aligned with the venture's financial projections and long-term strategic goals. Fundamentally, understanding the return on investment for every educational program or service allows edupreneurs to make informed decisions that promote fiscal sustainability while profoundly impacting lives through learning.

At its heart, edupreneurship marries the passion for educating with the precision of economics to create ventures capable of igniting minds and shaping futures. By comprehending and applying economic principles within education, edupreneurs can inspire learners and construct thriving businesses that serve as engines of innovation for the education sector. This synthesis of education economics empowers you to navigate the delicate balance between providing high-caliber educational experiences and managing the rigors of a competitive, evolving marketplace.

Revenue Models and Monetization Strategies lie at the heart of any edupreneurial venture, shaping the pathways through which innovation is transformed into tangible value. In the dynamic realm of education, where the thirst for knowledge meets the economics of supply and demand, understanding how to turn a profit while imparting education is critical.

One of the primary revenue models in edupreneurship is providing premium content. This can range from specialized courses and expert-led workshops to subscription services offering a continuously evolving learning library. The allure of exclusivity and high-quality material often opens the wallets of avid learners, and rightly so; the value accorded to education is evident in the outcomes it produces. How you craft your offerings—be they cerebral insights or practical skills—will influence your revenue stream directly.

Another approach is the freemium model, where foundational content is provided free of charge, with advanced features, tools, and learning experiences gated behind a paywall. This model invites learners into your ecosystem, allowing them to experience the value you create before they commit with their dollars. It's akin to sowing seeds that will, with the right nurturing, flourish into a garden of loyal paying subscribers. Remember, the freemium model's key is balance—you must offer enough value for free to captivate your audience yet reserve sufficient premium elements to incentivize upgrades.

Then there's the transactional model, wherein you design, market, and sell educational products—anything from e-books and lesson plans to full-blown curricula or educational software. Each sale brings revenue, and the focus shifts to volume and repeat customers. Diversifying your portfolio of educational products and knowing the pulse of your market will maximize revenue flows. Moreover, by creating a reputation for excellence and reliability in your educational product line, you cultivate a brand that stands out in a crowded marketplace.

Consulting and licensing present yet another avenue for monetization, particularly for those with a wellspring of expertise in specialized educational niches. Schools, educational institutions, or corporations may seek your acumen and be willing to pay for personalized advice, workshops, or the use of your intellectual property. Such engagements add to your revenue and enhance your credibility and visibility in the field of education.

No matter what monetization strategy you employ, let it be guided by the value you offer and the impact you wish to create. Align your financial aspirations with your mission to educate and empower; in doing so, you build a business that feels less like a venture and more like a vocation. As you ponder the most suitable revenue models for your enterprise, consider the intersection where passion for education meets the pragmatism of economics. Therein lies the sweet spot for edupreneurs to not only survive but thrive.

Financial Acumen for Edupreneurs is a pivotal cornerstone for those embarking on the transformative journey of molding the future through education and entrepreneurship. Edupreneurship isn't merely about possessing the ability to conceptualize and disseminate transformative educational experiences—it also demands a savvy understanding of the financial tides within which your vessel must sail. Approach your financial mastery with the same innovation and resilience that you apply to your pedagogical methods, understanding that in the confluence of educational value and financial health lies the longevity of your impact.

To navigate the financial streams successfully, internalize key notions of cash flow, investment, and cost structures. Recognize that each decision—whether selecting a platform for your content, hiring talent, or investing in marketing—has a financial pulse beating the rhythm of return on investment (ROI). Yet, never lose sight of the intrinsic value that education holds. Balance immediate monetary gains with the enduring effect of quality learning experiences. This intricate dance between fiscal prudence and educational richness is one you'll learn to perfect over time.

Effective budgeting weaves a coherent narrative around your financial choices, creating an architecture that supports growth while maintaining a safety net for unforeseen challenges. To this end, foresee the ebb and flow of educational demand using adaptive budgeting techniques that prepare you for seasonal fluctuations in your income. Embrace financial tools and software to track and analyze your financial health, allowing data to illuminate pathways for judicious spending, investment, and, when necessary, cost-cutting.

Funding, a crucial puzzle in the edupreneur's journey, requires attentiveness and adept storytelling abilities to attract the right investors and secure grants or loans. Your educational mission and a sound financial strategy are compelling tales that persuade stakeholders of your venture's viability. Transitioning from ideation to a financially sustainable operation often hinges on the clarity, confidence, and precision of your financial projections and fundraising initiatives.

Finally, let the concept of scalability sit at the core of your financial strategy. A sustainable educational endeavor anticipates growth and is designed to expand without sacrificing quality or financial stability. Foreplan how you will manage increasing costs and revenue, all while ensuring that your educational impact proliferates. With a firm grip on the financial helm, your edupreneurial ship will navigate tranquil and turbulent waters, steering towards a horizon where education and economic viability exist in fruitful harmony.

Budgeting, Financial Planning, and Securing Funding are at the heart of turning imaginative educational concepts into sustainable, impactful businesses. It's a pillar that holds up the architectural masterpiece that is your edupreneurial venture, and neglecting this can topple even the most innovative ideas. Proper financial planning demands a clear-eyed view of not only where your resources are coming from and where and how they're being used. As an edupreneur, you are tasked with charting every dollar's journey to ensure your venture's growth and longevity.

Let's demystify budgeting first. Envision your educational project as if it were a complex ecosystem—all parts are interdependent and vital for sustaining life. The budget is like the nutrient cycle; it ensures that resources reach where they're needed most and that nothing is wasted. Start by identifying all possible costs, from development expenses, marketing, technology, and materials to salaries, benefits, and contingency funds for unexpected needs. Assign a realistic value to each; this is not the time for whimsy—accuracy is your ally. With a robust budget in place, you have a firm foundation for your enterprise and a crucial tool for monitoring financial health.

With a well-crafted budget, your next move is strategic financial planning. This is where you step into the role of an architect, designing a blueprint that charts out future financial steps and anticipated monetary needs. It's about analyzing various scenarios, assessing risks, and preparing for potential financial challenges. Forecasting revenue streams, setting financial goals, and developing strategies for mitigating risk are essential exercises that enable you to steer through the economic uncertainties that any business venture may face. Don't just focus on surviving from month to month. Instead, envision a thriving enterprise that balances immediate financial necessities and long-term financial goals.

The pursuit of securing funding is akin to the quest for the Holy Grail for many edupreneurs. It's an essential quest that can bring your educational vision to fruition. There are various avenues for funding, each with its own challenges and rewards: from bootstrapping, crowdfunding, and angel investment to applying for educational grants and pitching to venture capitalists specializing in EdTech and social impact ventures. Present your enterprise not just as a business but as a mission-driven endeavor that has the potential to enhance educational outcomes and enrich lives. Your passion and preparation can be the key to unlocking financial support from investors who are eager to back revolutionary educational initiatives.

Remember, securing funding is not an end—it's a means to accompany you along the path of building and scaling your venture. Funding allows you to broaden your impact, refine your products, and invest in key areas that can make all the difference, such as research, development, and user experience. Maintaining comprehensive records and exercise transparency is imperative, as these practices will instill confidence in your funders and support you in securing additional funding if needed.

Financial vigilance is now your closest confidante. With a clear vision supported by realistic budgeting, strategic financial planning, and funded aspirations, your edupreneurial journey isn't just a hopeful foray but a well-prepared expedition toward meaningful impact in the educational space. An enterprise built on the bedrock of financial savvy is meant not just to survive but to thrive and, in doing so, transform the landscape of learning for generations to come.

Chapter 7:
Leadership, Team Building, and Operational Excellence

In the grand tapestry of edupreneurship, the threads of leadership, team building, and operational excellence weave a firm foundation for success. True edupreneurial leadership is an art that harmonizes the vision with actionable strategy, inspiring others to believe in a shared educational mission. It's about sparking an entrepreneurial spirit within each team member, where every voice contributes to the symphony of innovation. This chapter underlines the importance of constructing a cohesive team whose members' diverse skills create a resilient ecosystem capable of navigating the dynamic landscape of educational entrepreneurship. Harnessing the collective strengths, edupreneurs sculpt a culture that thrives on creativity, accountability, and relentless pursuit of excellence.

Operational excellence, the engine of our vessel, demands a meticulous approach that integrates lean processes, continuous improvement, and a relentless focus on value delivery. One finds the rhythm of sustained productivity in the elegant dance of systems and processes. Edupreneurs steer their ventures through the waves of market changes and educational demands by instilling a culture that champions adaptability and efficiency. This chapter serves as a compass for those ready to embark on this crucial aspect of their journey, illuminating the path to structure a venture that doesn't merely survive the tides of change but thrives within them.

Luis R. Valentino, Ed.D.

Edupreneurial Leadership and Team Building As the journey through the edupreneurial landscape forges ahead, leadership and team building emerge as cornerstones for creating and sustaining innovative educational ventures. Leadership in this context goes beyond the traditional management paradigms; it requires a blend of vision, passion, and an innate understanding of the educational milieu. The edupreneur acts as a beacon and catalyst, conceiving ideas and galvanizing a team to bring those ideas into reality. Fostering a collaborative environment where creativity and innovation thrive is pivotal. Such a leader recognizes that each team member's voice holds value, cultivating a setting where feedback and open communication are encouraged and integral to the venture's growth and adaptability.

Building a team in an edupreneurial setting demands a keen eye for talent that aligns with the venture's ethos and objectives. It's about finding individuals who are not only skilled but also share a commitment to transforming education. Diversity in a team goes a long way in enriching the educational products or services offered, as varied perspectives lead to a more comprehensive understanding of the needs of the market. However, assembling the team is only the beginning; the edupreneur must nurture a sense of shared purpose and ensure each team member is positioned to excel in their role. Effective team building leverages the strengths of its members, building a resilient framework capable of withstanding the challenges that the edupreneurial path presents.

Communication is the lifeblood of any high-functioning team, and in edupreneurship, it's essential for maintaining alignment on goals and expectations. Regular, transparent communication fosters trust and prevents misunderstandings, ensuring everyone moves in the right direction. It facilitates the flow of ideas, encourages the sharing of insights, and helps identify potential issues before they become hindrances. Communication within an edupreneurial team should not be a hierarchy but rather a multidirectional conversation that recognizes the unique contributions of each individual.

Conflict resolution skills are a must-have for the edupreneur. Conflict, when managed effectively, can be a gateway to innovation. It challenges the status quo and pushes the team to find unique solutions that might not have been considered otherwise. The edupreneurial leader must master the art of navigating disagreements with emotional intelligence, ensuring they become opportunities for growth rather than sources of fragmentation. This skill set is founded on listening actively, empathizing with team members, and constructively integrating different viewpoints into a unified, forward-moving strategy.

Finally, the true measure of edupreneurial leadership and team-building effectiveness lies in the team's output: innovative educational solutions that resonate with learners and educators alike. The edupreneur must be a steward of both people and purpose, continuously fostering development and recognizing the accomplishments of the team. Celebrating milestones, however small, reinforces camaraderie and commitment to the shared vision. As the team evolves, so should the leader, embodying the principles of lifelong learning and ongoing personal and professional growth. It's through this dynamic interplay of leadership and collaboration that edupreneurship carves out new paths in the world of education.

Operational Excellence in Edupreneurship reaches beyond the creation and delivery of educational content. It lies at the heart of sustainability and scalability, serving as the sturdy spine of any edupreneurial venture. Picture this: seamless processes, precise management, and an unrelenting focus on delivering value to the learner, all orchestrated with the dexterity of a conductor leading a symphony. Such harmony in operations can amplify impact and underline the credibility of education-focused enterprises.

Operational excellence can't be left to chance in an arena where every interaction counts. It starts with crystalline clarity in defining procedures and protocols. Edupreneurs must be minutely attuned to their venture's heartbeat – the workflow, the checkpoints, and the feedback loops that enkindle continuous improvement. By instituting rigorous standards and systematic methods, one ensures the learners' satisfaction and success and the educational team's efficiency and effectiveness. It's a multi-tiered endeavor, where adopting best practices isn't a one-time act but an ongoing journey of refinement and evolution.

Automation and delegation are indispensable threads in this fabric. With judicious technology utilization, routine tasks can be automated, liberating precious human capital to wrestle with more strategic objectives, such as curriculum innovation or market expansion. Delegation, enshrined within an accountability structure, empowers team members, catalyzing leadership and promoting ownership. Edupreneurs must aspire to instruct and inspire, fostering an environment where each team member can emerge as a champion driving the enterprise forward.

But operational excellence isn't all about systems and strategies. It's equally about responsiveness to the market's pulse. Agile methodologies allow edupreneurs to pivot with purpose, adapting their offerings in tandem with shifting educational needs and preferences. By keeping an ear close to the ground—to the whisperings of learners, educators, and industry trends—edupreneurs can fluidly adjust their sails and harness the winds of change. This responsiveness becomes a critical differentiation factor, setting apart the truly impactful ventures from the transient trends.

The bedrock of operational excellence, ultimately, is a relentless pursuit of quality and an unwavering commitment to the learner's journey. It's about instilling confidence, nurturing trust, and delivering outstanding value with each educational interaction. The edupreneur who masters this delicate dance of operational finesse positions their venture not just for success but for meaningful, long-term contributions to the evolution of education. They rise not as mere participants in the field but as architects of advancement, champions of change, and pioneers of a brighter educational paradigm.

Hiring, Managing Teams, and Fostering a Culture of Innovation Within the dynamic field of edupreneurship, the strength and creativity of your team can be your greatest asset. At the core of every successful educational venture lies a group of skilled individuals who are deeply aligned with the mission to transform education. Hiring is not just about filling a vacancy; it's a strategic endeavor to onboard individuals with specialized abilities who add to your enterprise's collective intelligence and drive. A judicious blend of talents is essential, from educators who understand the pulse of learning to tech wizards who can translate visionary ideas into tangible, user-friendly products.

In managing these teams, you must adopt a leadership style that is both collaborative and empowering. It's essential to rise above traditional hierarchies to create a space where each member feels invested in the growth and success of the organization. As you guide and mentor your team, practice active listening, demonstrate emotional intelligence, and cultivate an environment where feedback is accepted and encouraged. Flexibility is central; in the rapidly evolving landscape of education, adapting to change and encouraging your team to suggest innovative solutions can yield breakthroughs that set your venture apart.

However, fostering a culture of innovation is non-negotiable to unlock your team's potential. This is a milieu where out-of-the-box thinking is the norm, where failure is seen not as a setback but as a valuable step in the learning process. Celebrate creative risk-taking and allow your team the autonomy to experiment and explore new territories. By embracing cross-disciplinary collaboration and continually injecting fresh perspectives into projects, you create a fertile ground for innovation. Remember, the brightest ideas often spark at the intersection of diverse thoughts and disciplines.

Beyond traditional training and development programs, encourage your team to stay abreast with the latest trends, pedagogical strategies, and technological advancements. Provide them with opportunities to attend workshops, conferences, and industry events. This not only ensures that your team remains on the cutting edge but also signals your investment in their professional growth – a crucial factor in attracting and retaining top talent. Additionally, developing a shared vision and clear communication channels will ensure that everyone is pulling in the same direction, towards common goals.

Ultimately, the weave of your organization's fabric depends on the threads of trust, enthusiasm, and mutual respect that run through your team. A culture where ideas can be voiced without fear, where innovation is the expectation – this is where edupreneurs can truly blossom. It's not just about leading a team; it's about orchestrating a symphony of diverse talents to create learning solutions that resonate across the fabric of society, now and into the future.

Chapter 8:
Navigating Legalities and Ethics

Embarking on the journey of edupreneurship requires more than innovation and determination; it mandates a profound understanding of the intertwined legal and ethical landscapes underpinning education. As you forge from establishing the core of your edupreneurial venture to ensuring its longevity, the complexities of the law and the subtleties of ethics become your compass and anchor. You must become adept at protecting the intellectual sweat equity inherent in your educational products while simultaneously guaranteeing that the sanctity of privacy and ethical engagement for your learners remains inviolate. As you cultivate valuable partnerships and collaborations that propel your venture forward, an informed awareness of these legal and ethical considerations is not merely recommended—it's essential. This vigilance in upholding the highest standards will not only safeguard your enterprise but will also cement its reputation as a beacon of trust and integrity in the dynamic landscape of education.

Legal and Ethical Foundations In the realm of edupreneurship, understanding the bedrock of legal and ethical practices isn't simply about compliance; it's about cultivating trust, ensuring longevity, and building a brand that resonates with integrity. As you chart your course through the exciting waters of educational innovation, it's crucial to have your legal compass calibrated. Begin with a fundamental understanding of the laws related to educational content, such as copyright, licensing, and distribution. Stay abreast of the latest developments and seek professional advice when necessary—your legal foundation is as much a part of your business as the product you offer.

Consider ethics to be the heartbeat of your endeavor. Ethical considerations encompass more than the legally required; they involve the moral compass guiding decisions large and small. This includes how you treat the intellectual property of others, the transparency with which you communicate with customers and stakeholders, and how you handle your learners' personal data. Developing and maintaining a code of ethics safeguards your enterprise and serves as a beacon, attracting those who share or admire your values.

In the context of digital learning environments, pay particular attention to data privacy and protection. The educational sector often involves sensitive information, and regulations like the Family Educational Rights and Privacy Act (FERPA) in the United States underscore the importance of safekeeping student information. Clear, concise privacy policies and user agreements are not just legal requirements but declarations of your commitment to your users' security and privacy. Treat every piece of data with the highest respect and transparency; this practice will set you apart in the digital realm.

Furthermore, intellectual property (IP) is the lifeblood of an ecopreneur's offering. It's paramount to understand how to protect your original content, from lesson plans to online courses, and navigate using third-party materials responsibly. While IP law can be complex, it provides the structure that enables creativity to flourish without fear of misappropriation. Remember that your IP strategy should be defensive to protect your work from unauthorized use and offensive in that it allows you to carve out space in the market.

When forging collaborations and partnerships, the threads of legal and ethical considerations weave a strong tapestry. Enter each agreement with a thorough understanding of rights, responsibilities, and expectations. Ensure that every partnership is anchored by fair and equitable agreements that honor the contributions and interests of all parties involved. This approach will pave the way for fruitful collaborations and enhance your reputation as an edupreneur who values justice and mutual respect.

Protecting Intellectual Property In the innovative world of edupreneurship, your intellectual property (IP) is not just an asset—it's the very heart of your venture. This insightful facet of your business builds on the unique educational content, programs, and methodologies you've developed. As you disseminate knowledge and create tools to empower others, it's paramount that you safeguard your creations from infringement.

Understanding the landscape of IP rights equips you with the armor necessary to defend your work. There are several varieties of protection, each suited to different types of educational materials. Copyrights can safeguard your curricula, written works, and original content, assuring that your authorship is recognized and unauthorized distribution is controlled. Trademarks can protect your brand's distinguishing features—the name of your venture or a unique series within your educational offerings. Patents, although less commonly applicable in the field of education, might come into play if you've invented a new educational tool or process.

The quest for robust IP protection commences with a clear understanding of what is protectable and the criteria involved. Not everything can be ensconced under the IP umbrella. The barrier of creativity and originality must be met; your work must exhibit sufficient distinction to merit protection. As you weave your innovations into the fabric of education, consider embedding IP considerations into your planning from the outset. This entails keeping detailed records of your creation process, as contemporaneous documentation can be a bulwark in your defense should your ownership ever come into question.

Yet, being a steward of your own IP goes beyond the halls of registration offices; it's about vigilance and enforcement. In an arena like education, where sharing knowledge is foundational, striking a balance between dissemination and commercialization is key. Licensing agreements can allow others to use your materials while ensuring that your rights—and revenue streams—are intact. Be transformative in your thinking, just as you are transformative in your teaching; consider how your work can reach broader audiences while still maintaining the integrity and value of your IP.

Lastly, in the communal spirit of edupreneurship, don't merely shield your IP from the world; also respect the IP of others. This ethical standpoint will bolster your reputation and can lead to synergistic collaborations that enhance the educational landscape rather than merely extracting value from it. Your finesse in protecting your intellectual property secures your legacy in the dynamic expanse of education and enriches the entire ecosystem by setting a precedent for integrity and respect. You set the stage for your edupreneurial endeavor to flourish through meticulous IP management, crafting a beacon of inspiration for others to follow suit.

Privacy and Ethics in Education As we continue our exploration into the pillars of edupreneurship, it's imperative to turn the lens toward the critical issues of privacy and ethics within the educational space. Navigating the intersection of these values with business innovation requires a refined understanding of legal constraints and the moral imperatives that guard the sanctity of learning. In an age where digital footprints are indelible and personal data can be as valuable as currency, the onus rests on edupreneurs to become champions of privacy and stalwarts of ethical conduct.

In the realm of education, where sensitive student information and educational records are commonplace, strict adherence to privacy laws such as the Family Educational Rights and Privacy Act (FERPA) in the United States provides a baseline. However, the true edupreneurial spirit calls for going beyond compliance. It requires building trust through transparent practices and clear communication about collecting, using, and protecting student data. This trust is the currency of the educational market, as it can't be bought but must be earned daily through consistent, ethical action.

Ethics in education encompasses a broad spectrum of issues, including avoiding conflicts of interest, ensuring accessibility for all learners, and upholding the integrity of academic content. Edupreneurs must question not just what they can do with technology and data but also what they should do. The digital tools and platforms at the disposal of today's innovators come with the power to influence learning outcomes. With this power comes the responsibility to avoid manipulative practices and ensure that the technology empowers, not exploits, the learner.

Moreover, in the staging of educational products and services, edupreneurs must be vigilant in protecting the intellectual property rights of content creators while fostering a culture of respect and fair use. Striking a balance between innovation and respect for intellectual labor is crucial. As education becomes more open and collaborative, knowledge-sharing must coincide with honoring and recognizing the contributions of educators and thought leaders whose work underpins new educational ventures.

Privacy and ethics are not just checkboxes to be ticked or legal hurdles to be cleared on the path to edupreneurial success; they represent the foundation upon which sustainable and socially responsible businesses can grow. By embedding these principles into the DNA of an educational enterprise, edupreneurs set themselves apart in an increasingly crowded marketplace. They secure a competitive edge and contribute to a legacy of integrity that informs the transformative power of education. As we venture into uncharted territories of learning innovation, let these beacons of privacy and ethics guide our course, ensuring that the learning journeys we craft are as honorable as they are groundbreaking.

Crafting Collaborations and Partnerships As we venture into the heartlands of edupreneurship, one finds that forging robust collaborations and strategic partnerships is integral to cultivating a thriving educational enterprise. These alliances stretch beyond mere networking; they are the crucibles within which innovation and impact are seamlessly joined. Whether it is a burgeoning startup looking for expert guidance or an established entity seeking to expand its educational reach, grappling with the skill of partnership building is not just beneficial—it's essential.

In the educational landscape, partnerships equip edupreneurs with a symbiotic synergy. Imagine tapping into the resources and audiences of complementary organizations or harnessing collective expertise to create multifaceted learning solutions. The key is identifying partners who share the vision of transforming education and align with one's values and educational ethos. To embark on this, you must craft a value proposition that appeals to your prospective partners and offers an unmistakable benefit to them. This enables a partnership that thrives on mutual growth and goal achievement.

Yet, even with impeccable synergy, articulating the terms and expectations of the collaboration is imperative. Clear agreements that outline each party's contributions, responsibilities, and benefit shares prevent future discord. Recall that, in education particularly, collaborations are often visible to your learners and hence should exemplify the highest standards of integrity and cooperation. Demonstrate due diligence by incorporating legal agreements that respect intellectual property rights and clearly define the scope of the partnership to maintain a transparent and trusting relationship.

Moreover, the most impactful partnerships are those that are nurtured over time. This involves regular communication, setting joint milestones, and celebrating successes together. Continuous nurturing ensures the partnership evolves and adapts to the changing educational environment. Stay responsive to feedback from the partner and the learners experiencing this collaboration's outcome. An agile approach to collaborations allows for refinements that accommodate the dynamic nature of education and the market in which you operate.

Finally, assess and reflect on the success of your partnerships with a critical eye. Track the progress and outcomes with quantitative metrics and qualitative insights. By assessing the impact of the collaboration, you will learn valuable lessons that will inform your future ventures in the rich terrain of edupreneurship. Edupreneurs who master the art of crafting collaborations and partnerships set themselves apart by amplifying their offerings and extending their influence, ultimately catalyzing a greater educational change.

Chapter 9:
Measuring Impact and Scaling Your Venture

In the grand journey of nurturing your edupreneurial venture, you've laid the groundwork, sparked interest, and embraced the holistic framework of transformative education. As you stand at the crossroads of growth and expansion, Chapter 9 delves into the art and science of Measuring Impact and Scaling Your Venture. It's about transcending the superficial metrics, seeking responses that reflect true learning, and embedding continuous improvement into your venture's DNA. Evaluating impact isn't just about numbers; it's a narrative that includes your learners' voices, your community's engagement, and the positive changes sown within education. Furthermore, scaling is more than spread; it's an intentional, thoughtful process. A balance must be struck between steadfastness and adaptability, ensuring the core mission amplifies without diluting its essence. You'll learn to dream bigger and operationalize those dreams into strategies that traverse borders and cultures, establishing your venture as a beacon of global edupreneurial success. Your venture's reach can extend far and wide, potentially shaping education policy and reshaping learning landscapes, but this reach must be managed carefully and strategically. This chapter is your compass and map—prepare to chart a course toward tangible impacts and thoughtful scaling, heeding the call to transform the educational world.

Measuring Success and Impact

As we traverse the terrain of edupreneurship, let's pivot to the compass that guides us: measuring success and impact. To thrive as an edupreneur, it's not merely about profit margins and market share; it's profoundly about the footprints we leave in the sands of educational transformation. Success, in this arena, takes on a multilayered complexion — blending the quantitative with the qualitative, the financial returns with the learning outcomes, and the things we can count on with the changes we perceive in the lives of our learners. Therefore, measuring success encompasses a broad spectrum, from the robustness of a product's adoption to its rippling effects on educational practices and individual growth.

The metrics of measurement should be as versatile as the educational resources provided. Engagement levels, user feedback, and product longevity speak volumes about the practical effectiveness of your offerings. The true barometer of success lies in the evidence of learning gains; when your product, service, or solution uplifts knowledge, skills, and attitudes, you're on the right path. Standardized test scores, course completion rates, and the ability to demonstrate learned concepts in real-world scenarios offer tangible proof of your venture's impact. Yet, the intricate tapestries of personal success stories, peer recognition, and community testimonials weave the intricate human element into your edupreneurial narrative. These stories become not only our testimonials but also our living legacy.

As the architect of change, one must recognize that impact echoes far beyond the initial reverberations. Establishing a feedback loop that listens and learns from each educational encounter is crucial. Continuous improvement is fueled by this feedback, and through surveys, focus groups, and data analytics, we gain invaluable insights that enable us to fine-tune our offerings for greater resonance and reach. The focus on a sustainable, long-term impact thus transforms the journey of an edupreneur into a quest for a substantive difference in the educational landscape.

The summation of an ecopreneur's achievements isn't confined to their own growth but is equally measured by their contribution to the larger ecosystem of learning. Expanding access, dismantling barriers to education, and tailoring learning to diverse needs are all signs of a venture transcending traditional notions of success. On this continuum, influence becomes the new currency for the edupreneur, and their work serves as a beacon for future educational pioneers to follow.

Embracing this multifaceted approach to assessing our impact allows edupreneurs to paint a complete picture of their contribution. Aim high, and let the goals stretch beyond the tangible. We're in the business of molding minds and hearts, and that's a responsibility that comes with its own set of rewards. In this relentless pursuit of empowering others through education, we measure our success and impact and forge an enduring legacy that continues to inspire and ignite the flames of curiosity and learning across generations.

Scaling Strategies for Edupreneurs When embarking on the journey from launching an education-based venture to driving its growth, understanding effective scaling strategies is crucial. To expand your reach and impact as an edupreneur, you must refine your existing operations while identifying avenues for amplification. Growth is not just about numbers; it's about ensuring your educational offerings continue to resonate and provide value as they reach a broader audience. A well-thought-out scaling strategy is integral to a sustainable and successful edupreneurial pursuit.

First and foremost, consider the expansion of your educational products or services through diversification. This means adding complementary offerings that align with your core mission and meet emerging needs within the education landscape. Anticipate where the market is headed and what your learners might need next. This could involve creating advanced courses, offering new subjects, or integrating technology in innovative ways that enrich the learning experience. Continuous evolution, driven by a keen sense of curiosity and dedication to education, positions edupreneurs at the forefront of the industry's growth.

Furthermore, scaling requires a solid operational framework. Before you multiply your efforts, streamline your current processes. Automation and delegation are key. Investing in robust systems to manage increased demand ensures your venture can handle growth without compromising quality. As you delegate, hiring and nurturing a team that shares your vision and possesses the adaptability to thrive in a dynamic environment is crucial. Collective effort and shared leadership can elevate a venture from a one-person show to a symphony of collaborative innovation, bringing your educational vision to new heights.

Partnerships and collaborations offer another route to scaling your edupreneurial vision. You can combine resources, expertise, and networks to expand your venture's scope and scale by aligning with other organizations, individuals, or educational institutions. Strategic partnerships should be symbiotic, sharing an ethos of impact and a commitment to learners' success. Tread the path of collaboration with a clear vision and a well-defined set of mutual goals, and you'll find the journey to scaling can be accelerated and its outcome more fruitful.

Last but not least, an understanding of scale wouldn't be complete without addressing the digital realm. Establish a commanding online presence and leverage the global reach of digital marketing to promote your educational services. The power of social media, content marketing, and online communities should not be underestimated. Your digital footprint can break geographical barriers, allowing you to connect with a global audience and cultivate an international community of learners. Yet, with such potential for reach, it remains imperative to maintain a focus on quality, personalization, and meaningful engagement, ensuring that as your venture grows, it remains true to its educational core.

Scaling an edupreneurial venture is a journey of continual learning and adaptation. Stay attuned to the pulse of your market, maintain a clear strategic vision, and embrace the inevitability of change. Your capacity to scale and impact the world of education hinges on the balance between grand aspirations and grounded, meticulous execution. With tenacity and thoughtful scaling strategies, your edupreneurial venture can transform the educational landscape, making significant waves in the ocean of learning opportunities.

Going Global: Crossing Borders and Cultures Embarking on a journey beyond the confines of one's own culture requires deep insight, impeccable strategy, and an earnest understanding of our diverse world. As edupreneurs, the vision is to thrive within our local communities and spread the seeds of knowledge across the global landscape. The leap from local to international markets holds the potential to be profoundly rewarding. Your educational innovation, be it a curriculum, technology, or unique learning methodology, can resonate with audiences far beyond your initial scope—if adapted with cultural intelligence and global awareness.

The process of crossing borders in education is a delicate dance with nuance and respect. Begin by recognizing that educational needs and preferences vary drastically among different populations. Your content must be as fluid as the learners it seeks to empower, capable of transforming in ways that preserve its core ethos while respecting the traditions and customs of new learners. Educators diving into international waters must fine-tune their products to achieve relevance and resonance. This act ensures material is not just accessible but also meaningful across varying cultural contexts, languages, and educational systems.

Expanding globally necessitates not only translation but also transcreation. Your message should carry the same motivational spark in each new language it adopts. Collaborate with local experts to maintain the nuance and integrity of your content within each culture. This partnership brings forth a level of authenticity that can't be achieved through translation alone and avoids potential missteps that could derail your venture's acceptance and success. Moreover, technology plays a crucial role, allowing edupreneurs to leverage platforms and tools that facilitate seamless integration and delivery worldwide.

Building trustworthy relationships is also pivotal when crossing borders. This involves immersing one's self in the local education community, understanding regulatory hurdles, and conforming to various learning environments. Networking with local influencers and decision-makers can unlock doors that might otherwise remain closed. It's not solely about selling a product but about creating a movement that aligns with the ambitions and aspirations of learners worldwide. Networking also opens the door to potential collaboration, which can significantly enhance the depth and reach of your offerings while fostering innovation through diverse perspectives.

In conclusion, taking your educational venture global is an endeavor that demands adaptability, cultural empathy, and strategic collaboration. It's about creating bridges where gaps exist and fashioning a learning environment that transcends traditional boundaries. As you extend your influence, remember that the power of education lies in its ability to unite and inspire, irrespective of geographical borders. With a mindful approach to crossing cultures, your venture can be a catalyst for inclusive growth and a beacon of knowledge for learners around the globe.

Chapter 10:
The Future of Edupreneurship and Personal Growth

As we gaze into the horizon of education's evolution, the fusion of entrepreneurship and pedagogical savvy promises a vibrant future teeming with possibilities. The tapestry of edupreneurship weaves together the richness of personal development with the pragmatism required to navigate the educational marketplace of tomorrow. Within this emergent landscape, one finds opportunities to innovate, contribute to societal learning, and embark on a profound journey of self-improvement and discovery. It's a future where the growth of the individual mirrors the growth of their ventures, a symbiotic ecosystem where passion for education fuels the relentless pursuit of knowledge and self-refinement. As edupreneurs, stepping into this future means embracing the relentless pace of change, harnessing it as a catalyst for business agility and personal enlightenment. It envisions a world where learning and growth are not destinations but rather perennial states of being, as integral to life as breathing. In this boundless context, edupreneurs are poised to thrive, their ventures a testament to the transformative power of marrying educational innovation with tireless self-evolution.

The Future of Education and Edupreneurship envisions a landscape where learning is not confined to physical classrooms or traditional curriculums. As educators and business leaders, the horizon stretches beyond what we see today; it calls for a deep dive into an era where education melds seamlessly with entrepreneurship. Imagine a realm where flexibility, innovation, and personalized learning pathways are not just ideals but everyday practice. The transformation is underway, and the trailblazers of this shift are the edupreneurs—visionaries who recognize that the capacity for learning should have no bounds and that the experience of education can be phenomenally enriched through entrepreneurial spirit.

Yet, what does this future look like when painted with the brush of possibility? It's a canvas where technology and humanity converge, creating an ecosystem where learners of all ages can pursue knowledge and skills in ways that captivate their individual passions and learning styles. In this domain, edupreneurs are the architects of pioneering platforms and experiences that cater to a global audience. They tap into the vast potential of online resources, leverage artificial intelligence to personalize learning and employ data analytics to refine educational offerings continuously. Such a prospect requires a grasp of technological tools and an insightful understanding of learners' diverse and evolving needs.

Entering the educational arena necessitates an unwavering commitment to reshaping and reimagining the status quo. The shift toward learner-centric models drives innovation, urging educators and entrepreneurs to craft solutions that address genuine problems in education systems worldwide. This might involve harnessing gamification to transform mundane subjects into engaging quests or building collaborative networks that tear down geographical barriers to quality teaching. Edupreneurs who thrive in this space possess a kaleidoscope of skills—merging creative thought with solid business acumen, identifying niches, and embedding a value-driven ethos into their pursuits while maintaining the delicate balance between profitability and social impact.

Moreover, the social fabric of education is changing, giving rise to communities of learning where the exchange of knowledge is not unidirectional but a shared experience. From crowd-sourced learning materials to interactive forums powered by the collective intelligence of educators across the globe, the community's role in education is more integral than ever. Edupreneurs are at the forefront, fostering these connections and creating environments where learners not only consume content but contribute to the collective wisdom of their peers.

As we peer into the not-so-distant future, it's clear that the role of the edupreneur is multidimensional and full of opportunities yet to be uncovered. They are not just educators or businesspeople—they are catalysts for change, equipped with the fortitude to break new ground in the quest for educational excellence. With each learner's success, they reaffirm the boundless potential of education fueled by entrepreneurial drive. The metamorphosis of education is in their hands, and as stewards of the next wave of educational ingenuity, they're just getting started.

Case Studies of Successful Edupreneurial Ventures Case studies of successful edupreneurial ventures provide us with a comprehensive understanding of the concept of edupreneurship, showcasing the possibilities, challenges, and potential successes that can be achieved through innovative and determined efforts. By examining these real-life examples, we can gain valuable insights into the complexities of launching and growing a successful education-focused venture.

These narratives highlight the importance of identifying educational needs, developing innovative solutions, and executing strategic plans while also shedding light on the potential obstacles and setbacks that may arise along the way. Through a deep analysis of these cases, we can develop a well-rounded understanding of the opportunities and challenges of being an edupreneur, ultimately inspiring and guiding others to embark on their own successful ventures.

Gary Surdam is the President/CEO of Brightspot International Education (brightspoteducation.com). his programs are global and cover a number of areas, including STEAM education, entrepreneurship, career education, international student success, and teacher training. He has had a long and successful career in education, spanning over 30 years as both a teacher and an edupreneur. Gary's journey in the education industry began in 1995 when he realized he wanted to do more to help students, teachers, and parents. At the time, he was not focused on becoming an edupreneur but rather on making a difference in the lives of as many students as possible.

Gary's mindset has always been centered on helping students, teachers, and administrators. He began his venture in a small program called the Apprentice Program, where he worked across multiple states to establish himself in his niche. After becoming established, he started his own company, which he later sold to the Chicago Tribune. Eventually, he bought it back and rebranded it. This time, the process was smoother because Gary had learned the importance of research, planning, and intentional execution.

Throughout his journey, Gary has faced many challenges, but he has also had those special moments he calls "sparks" that inspire and motivate him to keep moving to the next level. He advises those starting on a similar path to slow down, build a plan of action, and define their purpose. He emphasizes the importance of learning as much as possible and not looking for shortcuts, as success requires much hard work.

One of Gary's most critical lessons is learning about the foundations of edupreneurship and the niche he was pursuing. He stresses the importance of having a passion for the work, as the commitment required is significant. Additionally, he advises learning from those who have gone through the experience and setting short-term and long-term goals to help keep oneself moving forward.

Gary's wife and family have significantly contributed to his success. Without their support, he would not be where he is today. With the right mindset, instinct, and support system, anyone can build a successful venture that makes a difference in the lives of students, teachers, and administrators.

The path toward edupreneurship involves much more than starting a business in the education sector. It's about a deep commitment to our values, continuous learning, and the courage to pursue our vision authentically and resiliently. Educators can successfully transition to becoming edupreneurs and create impactful and fulfilling careers.

Dr. Sabba Quadwai is the CEO of Designing Schools (https://designingschools.org/). She is an expert and evangelist in artificial intelligence (AI). She describes her mission as giving educators the skills and strategies to build their human advantage and be irreplaceable in an AI-driven world. She has been serving schools and businesses using Design Thinking for the past decade.

Her journey exemplifies her transformative journey from educator to edupreneur. Her narrative serves as a guide for educators aspiring to embark on the path of edupreneurship, whether as a primary career or a supplementary endeavor. Through her experiences, Sabba illuminates the pathway for aspiring edupreneurs, providing insights and advice that underscore the necessity of resilience, innovation, and a deep-seated purpose to overcome challenges and reap substantial rewards.

From the outset of her edupreneurial journey, Sabba realized the significance of having a clear "why" to guide her efforts. This understanding wasn't merely motivational; it became the bedrock of her success for over a decade, driving her to identify and address educational gaps. She discovered that the essence of edupreneurship lies in knowing the "how" and pursuing the "why," a philosophy that fueled her pursuit of impactful educational solutions.

Sabba's journey was markedly shaped by her expertise in Design Thinking and her proactive pursuit of mentorship, which forged her unique edupreneurial niche. This dual approach of leveraging skill and guidance became the cornerstone of her development, laying the groundwork for her ambitions. She emphasizes the importance of continual learning and skill enhancement for those on the edupreneurial path, advocating for a diligent assessment of one's expertise and the cultivation of necessary competencies.

Her path to edupreneurship also became a voyage of self-discovery, allowing her to crystallize her values, define her venture's mission, and design products or services that authentically reflect her beliefs and capabilities. This introspection and alignment of personal values with her entrepreneurial vision underscore the essence of creating a venture that genuinely resonates with its intended audience.

For Sabba, the mindset has played a pivotal role in navigating the edupreneurial landscape. Although challenges punctuated her journey, her positive outlook and persistence enabled her to transform these hurdles into opportunities for growth and learning. She counsels edupreneurs to cultivate a mindset focused on continual improvement and resilience.

Moreover, she advises against conforming to inauthentic niches or styles. True edupreneurial success, she argues, stems from authentically representing one's beliefs and genuine engagement with one's audience. This authenticity fosters a relatable brand and builds a lasting connection with customers.

In essence, Sabba's edupreneurial narrative is a testament to the power of purpose, persistence, and authenticity in crafting a meaningful and successful venture in the educational landscape. Her story serves as a beacon for aspiring edupreneurs, guiding them through the intricacies of transforming educational passion into impactful edupreneurship.

Tom Davis is Director of Business Development at The Center for Educational Innovation. Tom's journey from the classroom to the business world is a testament to the power of ambition, risk-taking, and a deep-seated desire to make a difference. After 15 years of teaching, financial reasons prompted him to consider a career shift. As a bilingual teacher, he had gained valuable experience in curriculum development and individualization, but he always felt there was something more he could do for his students. This led him to the world of entrepreneurship, a path he was naturally inclined towards as a risk-taker.

His first "side hustle" was grant writing, which he got involved in after writing an Eisenhower grant. This experience sparked his interest in educational technology and leadership, leading him to start a comprehensive STEAM program. The transition was nerve-wracking, as any career change would be, but the potential of transforming education drove him.

Tom's edupreneurial journey began with roles in edtech sales and regional management, eventually leading to a position as vice president of sales. He focused on helping students who struggled with learning, particularly those at risk and with special needs in the STEAM field. Tom leveraged the extensive knowledge and experience he had developed as an educator to support his transition.

It took Tom fourteen years to start his own venture, which had challenges. When Tom went independent, he planned his transition carefully, ensuring he had a steady income and a clear understanding of the cash flow needed. He also had to constantly work on building his potential client database, a crucial lesson he learned from Robert Miller's book Strategic Selling.

Despite the challenges, Tom's impact has been significant. He has helped companies build their assets by providing good products, believing it only helps to expand his dream of making a difference for our most marginalized students. His business model is grounded in the belief that you can make a good income while making a positive difference. It takes hard work, continuous learning, and trusting relationships. In the end, it can lead to great success.

His advice to aspiring edupreneurs is to do their homework, ensure they have clarity on their chosen path, and remember that the edupreneurial space can be rewarding both financially and in terms of positive impact. His journey is a testament to the power of "ganas" - a deep desire to make a difference.

There are many more stories of educators embarking on impactful endeavors that actively contribute to the evolution of education. These stories encompass a wide range of initiatives, such as...

- a small tutoring service that blossomed into a leading online education platform. The founders identified a gap in accessible, quality tutoring for complex subjects and leveraged technology to connect learners with top-notch educators globally. They started with a simple website, offering a handful of courses, and by persistently iterating their approach based on learner feedback, they expanded their reach exponentially or,
- a company that began producing educational toys and games, which sparked curiosity and creativity among young minds. The founders started in their garage, meticulously handcrafting each item. Their brand gained trust through

community engagement and genuine storytelling that resonated with parents' desires for meaningful play. They scaled their operations, eventually partnering with schools and educational institutions to integrate their products into classrooms, revolutionizing how play and learning coexist or,

- former educators who saw the struggle of students with dyslexia. They created an app that combined artificial intelligence with language exercises to create a personalized learning experience. The unique selling point was the app's capacity to adapt to each user's pace, providing a sense of achievement and progress to students who previously felt left behind. Its success wasn't just measured in revenue but in the stories of improved literacy and self-esteem amongst its users or,

- a group of passionate teachers, recognizing the potential of their combined expertise, embarked on a journey to create a comprehensive toolbox of educational resources. By pooling their units and lessons, they curated a diverse collection tailored to meet the needs of educators across various subjects and grade levels. With the aim of supporting fellow teachers and enhancing student learning experiences, they decided to make their meticulously crafted toolbox available for purchase on online platforms, thereby sharing their knowledge and expertise with a wider audience or,

- the remarkable venture that connected remote communities with the world through a network of innovative learning centers. These centers, equipped with solar-powered technology and internet connectivity, offered courses in partnership with global experts to bring quality education to the most underserved areas. The impact went beyond academia, fostering community development and providing a model for sustainable edupreneurship that blends purpose with profit.

The landscape of education and business is ever-evolving, so staying informed and skilled is essential. This helps you refine your offering and adapt to changes and challenges. Embrace the complexity of your dreams and goals. Life and entrepreneurship are not about choosing one path over another but about integrating your passions into a coherent, fulfilling career. This means prioritizing and organizing your goals to complement each other and fit within the larger picture of your life and aspirations.

Personal Growth for the Edupreneur In the dynamic journey of edupreneurship, personal growth stands as one of the most critical elements for sustained success and fulfillment. As an edupreneur, you are forging educational pathways and constructing the architecture of your personal evolution. Often, personal and professional spheres intersect, making it essential for edupreneurs to invest in their development as both educators and business leaders.

This growth process makes cultivating an ever-expanding awareness of one's strengths and weaknesses paramount. Self-reflection is the cornerstone, enabling edupreneurs to resonate with their core values and align their mission with heartfelt authenticity. Equipped with this insight, one can navigate the landscape of education and business with heightened emotional intelligence and strategic acuity. You'll discover that personal growth reinforces professional endeavors, as each lesson learned and challenge surmounted contributes to your edupreneurial toolkit.

It is through the crucible of continuous learning that edupreneurs sharpen their acumen. Embracing lifelong learning is not just about industry trends or pedagogical methodologies but also about understanding human psychology, leadership dynamics, and the subtle art of influencing change. As you evolve, you become a beacon of inspiration, adopting a mindset of possibility that infects all areas of your life. With its peaks and valleys, your journey becomes a testament to resilience and adaptability—qualities that shine brightly in the ever-changing educational landscape.

Additionally, personal growth necessitates a balance between ambition and well-being. Pursuing edupreneurial success must not overshadow the need for physical, emotional, and spiritual health. In this fast-paced venture, recognize the importance of cultivating work-life harmony. Prioritizing self-care and setting boundaries ensures the longevity of your career and the richness of your personal life. This synergy supports a creative outpouring that is both prolific and sustainable, allowing you to serve your audience without sacrificing your essence.

Finally, the art of edupreneurship, for all its strategic and intellectual demands, thrives on the personal touch. As you grow, so too does your capacity to connect, empathize, and innovate. Personal growth fuels your vision, painting your educational products and services with the vivid colors of your unique journey. It forges a path of significance and impact and, above all, serves as the thread that weaves together the tapestry of edupreneurship—a tapestry stitched with the threads of knowledge, experience, and the indomitable human spirit.

Lifelong Learning, Work-life Harmony, and Self-care embody essential virtues for the consummate edupreneur. In the throes of crafting educational breakthroughs and nurturing transformative innovation, one must not lose sight of the importance of personal enrichment and equilibrium. Lifelong learning is the heartbeat of edupreneurship – it's an unwavering commitment to evolve intellectually and professionally amidst a rapidly changing world. Encouragingly, the passion for education that leads one to become an edupreneur simultaneously fuels a natural propensity for lifelong learning. By staying abreast of the latest trends, research, and methodologies within one's specialty and beyond, an edupreneur remains versatile and prepared to adapt their ventures in alignment with the needs and shifts of the educational landscape.

Yet, while professional growth invites copious rewards, it mustn't overshadow the quest for work-life harmony. The sphere of edupreneurship, often characterized by irregular hours, continual ideation, and unrelenting ambition, can blur the boundaries between personal and professional life. Here lies the artful challenge: maintaining a harmonic balance between the exhilaration of edupreneurial pursuit and the tranquility of personal life. This balance is not prescriptive; it's an individualized rhythm that allows each edupreneur to thrive without succumbing to burnout. It's the acknowledgment that to nourish the minds of others; one must also nourish their own body and soul with quality time for family, friends, hobbies, and rest.

Self-care is the personal health and well-being facet often relegated to an afterthought, yet it is crucially interwoven with lifelong learning and work-life harmony. Tethered to the essence of self-care is the understanding that one's physical, emotional, and mental health is the foundation upon which all else is built. Incorporating routine self-care practices into daily life enables edupreneurs to approach their endeavors with clarity, energy, and resilience. Whether through meditation, exercise, leisure reading, or a creative outlet, self-care strategies significantly contribute to a sustainable and fulfilling edupreneurial journey.

The interplay of lifelong learning, work-life harmony, and self-care constructs a robust platform for personal and professional fulfillment. They coalesce to ensure that edupreneurs can deliver their highest value to clients and students while cultivating a personally rewarding lifestyle. Robust educational ventures are frequently spearheaded by individuals who enthusiastically invest in their well-being and continuous improvement, manifesting their best selves in all facets of their endeavors.

For those embarking on or traversing the edupreneurial path, recognize that success is not solely measured by professional achievements but equally by the contentment and holistic growth realized along the journey. Lifelong learning widens one's horizon, work-life harmony enables joy and productivity to dance in sync, and self-care ensures the dance is performed with grace and longevity. Embrace these principles, weave them into the fabric of your edupreneurial tapestry, and watch as they enrich both the lives of those you aim to educate and your life in untold, splendid ways.

Paving the Road to Transformative Innovation

In this journey through the landscape of edupreneurship, we've explored myriad aspects that form the essence of innovative educational entrepreneurship. At its core, the message is one of transformation—a call to action for educators, leaders, and visionaries, fueling the drive toward impactful change in the realm of learning. Through cultivating a resilient mindset, recognizing rich opportunities, and understanding the nuanced needs of our learners, edupreneurs are uniquely positioned to revolutionize education.

Crafting educational products that resonate with today's learners mandates a blend of creativity, pedagogic insight, and business acumen. Every step, from the design phase to the launch runway, has been guided by the lean principles of testing, learning, and iterating—enabling you to sculpt educational experiences that are not just instructional but truly enlightening. By embracing technology, the innovative educator can extend the learning environment, making it more accessible, engaging, and tailored to individual needs, thus ushering forth an era where education is not seen as a privilege but a pervasive right.

Your edupreneurial venture is significant; it's a beacon that lights the path for others to follow. As you've journeyed through brand creation, ethical marketing, and community engagement, the takeaway is clear: transparency, authenticity, and social responsibility are not just buzzwords—they are the pillars upon which successful brands are built. Coupled with the strategic use of data and AI tools, these essentials will enable you to connect deeply with your community, garner trust, and forge a lasting impact.

However, the substance that supports any educational venture doesn't stop at the creative—it extends profoundly into the operational. Leadership, solid business practices, understanding of the economics of education, and mastery of the legalities encompass a holistic approach that ensures your venture is inspired and sustainable. This blending of creativity with management will ensure your venture will succeed and thrive even as it grows, scales, and meets the challenges of a constantly evolving marketplace.

As we conclude, remember that the road to transformative innovation is ongoing. It's paved with the bricks of continuous learning, personal growth, and an unwavering commitment to making a difference. Today's edupreneurs are the torchbearers, navigating through a dynamic educational topography, leading towards a future where learning is liberated from traditional constraints. This momentous quest you embark upon is more than a career; it's a crusade toward empowering minds and igniting potential. Stand poised at the threshold of possibility and, with thoughtful resolve, step forward into the luminous dawn of transformative innovation.

**Part 2
The Workbook**

Welcome to the companion workbook of "The Edupreneurs' Foundation: Principles of Educational Entrepreneurship." This workbook is an essential tool designed to bridge the gap between understanding and action. It serves as your personal incubator for the key concepts and ideas presented in the book, allowing you to translate theory into tangible strategies for your edupreneurial endeavors. Through carefully structured reflection spaces, brainstorming sections, and practical application exercises, you will be able to internalize and apply the knowledge you've gained. The inclusion of images aims to enhance your comprehension and inspire deeper insight. Our hope is that this workbook will not only equip you with the necessary skills but also instill the confidence to innovate and lead in the educational sphere. Embark on this journey with us, and let this workbook be the catalyst that prepares you to turn your edupreneurial visions into reality.

Introduction

Key Concepts

Edupreneurship is a concept that combines education and entrepreneurship. It's about using business principles and innovation to improve education.

Emergence and Significance:

- Traditional education is being challenged to evolve due to constant change and technology.
- Edupreneurs see gaps in the system and create businesses to address them, personalizing education and making it more accessible.
- They use creativity and business skills to deliver effective learning experiences.
- Edupreneurs are revolutionizing education through:
    - **Personalized learning**: Tailoring education to individual needs.
    - **Innovation:** Introducing new technologies and methods like VR, AI, and adaptive learning platforms.
    - **Democratization**: Making education more accessible through online courses and tools.

Impact

- Edupreneurship cultivates lifelong learners who can adapt to a changing world.
- It prepares society for a future of continuous learning and abundant opportunities.

History

- Edupreneurship has been evolving for decades, with roots in correspondence courses and educational publications.
- The rise of the internet significantly impacted edupreneurship by allowing educators to reach a global audience online.
- Early edupreneurs created online courses and showed education could be flexible and diverse.
- They disrupted the status quo by offering learner-driven, tech-based education models.
- Today, edupreneurship encompasses MOOCs, bootcamps, language apps, and personalized learning experiences.

Overall, edupreneurship is a powerful force that is transforming education by making it more effective, accessible, and relevant to the 21st century.

Chapter 1:
Cultivating the Edupreneurial Mindset

Edupreneurial Mindset:

- The edupreneurial mindset merges education and entrepreneurship, focusing on innovation and transformation in learning. It embodies foresight, adaptability, creativity, and a commitment to enhancing educational experiences.

- Edupreneurs see beyond conventional teaching methods and embrace disruption, building, and continuous evolution.

Defining Edupreneurship:

- Edupreneurship combines a passion for education with the innovative drive of entrepreneurship.

- Edupreneurs create educational opportunities that inspire and instruct, applying a business mindset to address educational needs and manifest change.

- Edupreneurs include teachers expanding beyond traditional classrooms, tech innovators developing educational apps, and founders of educational startups.

Characteristics of Successful Edupreneurs:

- Passion for education

- Perseverance and work ethic
- Adaptability
- Blend of educator's soul and businessperson's mind
- Strong communication and leadership skills

Cultivating an Innovative and Resilient Mindset:
- Curiosity and a passion for learning
- Embracing challenges as opportunities
- Seeking diverse perspectives
- Maintaining optimism and perseverance
- Emotional intelligence and stress management

Overcoming Common Challenges and Setbacks:
- Learning from failures and setbacks
- Maintaining a future-oriented mindset
- Adapting business models and teaching methodologies
- Importance of communication and collaboration
- Prioritizing self-care and continuous learning

Reflection of the Chapter

Let's keep in mind the concept of edupreneurial mindset and answer the following questions:

1. How do you define the edupreneurial mindset, and why is it crucial for modern education?

   _____

   _____

   _____

   _____

2. Reflect on a time when you saw a need for innovation in education. How did you respond, and how might an edupreneurial mindset have influenced your approach?

   _____

   _____

   _____

   _____

3. What educational opportunities do you see in your current environment that could benefit from an entrepreneurial approach?

   _____

   _____

   _____

   _____

4. How can the combination of a passion for education and a business mindset create impactful changes in the learning experience?

_____
_____
_____
_____
_____

Cultivating an Innovative and Resilient Mindset is all about Stepping outside familiar boundaries, encouraging experimentation, and fostering a culture of inquiry. viewing setbacks as learning opportunities and maintaining an optimistic outlook to persevere.

1. How do you currently foster innovation and creativity in your educational practice? What steps can you take to enhance this aspect further?

   _____
   _____
   _____
   _____
   _____

2. Describe a situation where you had to adapt quickly to changes in your educational environment. What strategies did you use, and how effective were they?

   _____
   _____
   _____
   _____
   _____

3. What are your long-term goals as an edupreneur, and how do they align with the evolving demands of society and the education market?

_____
_____
_____
_____
_____

Case Scenario Addressing Equity in Education

You are passionate about addressing educational inequities in underserved communities. You want to create a nonprofit organization that provides free educational resources and support to these communities.

1. How would you identify the most pressing educational needs in these communities?

   _____
   _____
   _____
   _____
   _____

2. What innovative solutions could you propose to address these needs, and how would you implement them?

   _____
   _____
   _____
   _____
   _____

3. How would you ensure that your organization remains financially sustainable while providing free services?

　_____
　_____
　_____
　_____
　_____

4. What metrics would you use to evaluate the impact of your nonprofit's efforts on educational outcomes in these communities?

　_____
　_____
　_____
　_____
　_____

Chapter 2:
Identifying Opportunities and Understanding Your Market

1. Recognizing Educational Opportunities:

Innovative Intersection: The chapter emphasizes the potential for innovation at the intersection of education and entrepreneurship. Identifying opportunities within this space requires a keen eye and strategic approach.

2. Spotting Opportunities in the Education Landscape:

Strategic and Intuitive Skills: Successful edupreneurs combine strategic thinking with intuition and a passion for education to identify and seize opportunities.

Underserved Niches: Identifying gaps in the current educational system, such as underserved communities or emerging trends, is crucial.

Digital Disruption: Recognizing how technological advancements can create new opportunities for educational innovation is essential.

Current Challenges as Opportunities: When traditional systems fail, gaps arise that can be filled with innovative solutions. This includes addressing specific learner needs, such as bespoke materials for students with disabilities or updated career-oriented programs.

3. Embracing Technological Advancements:

Role of Technology: Understanding and leveraging technology's role in education, such as AI, VR, mobile learning, gamification, and online collaboration tools, is critical.

Integration for Impact: Effective edupreneurs integrate these technological advancements in meaningful ways to add value to the learning process.

4. Engaging with the Educational Community:

Community Participation: Active engagement with the educational community through conversations, conferences, and professional groups helps refine opportunity-spotting skills.

Listening and Learning: Listening to educators and learners provides valuable insights into their pain points and needs, which can then be addressed through innovative solutions.

5. Understanding Your Learners:

Learner-Centric Approach: Learners are central to edupreneurial endeavors, and understanding their needs, motivations, and challenges is crucial.

Diverse Needs and Preferences: Recognizing the diverse needs of different learner segments, such as their goals, learning styles, and demographic factors, is essential for tailoring educational solutions.

6. Using Data to Drive Decision-Making:

Data as a Compass: Data-driven decision-making is a cornerstone of successful edupreneurship, guiding vision and ensuring evidence-based choices.

Quantitative and Qualitative Insights: Collecting and analyzing both quantitative and qualitative data helps tailor offerings to resonate with learners.

7. Exploring New Markets and Opportunities:

Beyond Conventional Boundaries: Successful edupreneurs look beyond obvious markets to identify unserved or underserved niches across different cultures, professions, and communities.

Technological Leverage: Utilizing online platforms and digital tools to reach previously inaccessible audiences expands the scope of educational ventures.

Reflection Questions

Edupreneurs must maintain a clear vision for education, using it as both a compass and anchor. By exploring new markets and continuously adapting to changing needs, they can capture opportunities and drive educational innovation.

To fully understand it, let us consider the case scenario of "Innovative Edupreneur Jack's Journey"

Jack, an enthusiastic edupreneur, identified a lack of quality online resources for high school students struggling with advanced mathematics. To address this gap, he created "MathMaster," a comprehensive online platform offering interactive video lessons, practice problems, and personalized tutoring using AI.

To validate his idea, Jack conducted focus groups and surveys with students and teachers, revealing a strong demand for his platform. He launched a beta version, partnering with a few local schools for a pilot program. Despite initial challenges with technology adoption and engagement, Jack's persistence paid off as the platform saw a significant improvement in students' math performance and interest.

Based on feedback, Jack continuously improved the platform, adding gamification elements and a mobile app. He also explored expanding his services to include other subjects and cater to different educational levels. Jack's venture gained recognition, leading to partnerships with educational institutions and non-profits.

Reflection:

1. How did Jack identify the need for an online mathematics resource? What methods did he use to validate his idea?

_____
_____
_____
_____
_____

2. Discuss how Jack used technology to create MathMaster. What technological features were key to its success?

_____
_____
_____
_____
_____

3. Evaluate Jack's approach to engaging with students and teachers during the development of MathMaster. How did this engagement impact the platform's design and effectiveness?

_____
_____
_____
_____

4. What challenges did Jack face during the initial launch of MathMaster? How did he address these challenges to ensure the platform's success?

_____
_____
_____
_____

5. What metrics should Jack use to measure the success of MathMaster? How can he ensure the platform continues to meet the needs of its users?

_____
_____
_____
_____

Chapter 3:
Developing and Testing Your Educational Product

Crafting the Educational Product:

- **Vision to Reality:** Transform your educational vision into a tangible product that merges creativity with analytical rigor.
- **Content Development:** Create engaging and pedagogically sound content, akin to a gardener pruning and refining until it's splendid.
- **Storytelling and Evidence-Based Results**: Combine storytelling with evidence-based results to make the content compelling and effective.

Iterative Development Process:

- **Test, Iterate, Enhance:** Introduce your product to a small audience, gather feedback, and continually refine it.
- **Feedback Loop**: Use critiques as insights to improve the product, ensuring it exceeds expectations.
- **Measuring Effectiveness**: Continuously measure and adjust the product to stay aligned with changing educational needs.

Designing Compelling Content:

- **Engagement and Educational Objectives**: Craft content that engages learners and meets clear educational objectives.

- **Scaffolding and Cognitive Roadmaps:** Develop a learning pathway that builds on prior knowledge and ensures deep understanding.

- **Real-World Applications:** Make learning relevant through practical applications like simulations, case studies, and hands-on projects.

Personalization and Adaptive Learning:

- **Differentiated Learning Paths**: Use data to create personalized learning experiences that cater to individual learner profiles.

- **Iterative Design**: Continuously test and refine the content based on user feedback to maintain a dynamic and evolving learning environment.

Lean Edupreneurship:

- **Agile Mindset**: Adopt an agile and adaptive approach, functioning like a lifelong learner constantly refining your product.

- **Minimum Viable Product (MVP):** Develop a simple, functional version of your product to test assumptions and gather early feedback.

- **Qualitative and Quantitative Feedback**: Use surveys, interviews, and observations to guide the iterative process and refine the product.

Creating Minimum Viable Products (MVPs):

- **Core Functionality**: Focus on the core value proposition that addresses the primary problem or need.

- **Feedback and Iteration**: Collect user feedback to inform improvements, ensuring the product evolves based on real-world interactions.

- **Educational Efficacy and Feasibility**: Balance educational effectiveness with technological feasibility, ensuring the product integrates seamlessly into existing educational systems.

Continuous Improvement and Adaptability:

- **Real-World Applications**: Use feedback from real-world applications to drive continuous improvement.

- **Practical and Accessible Solutions**: Ensure the product is practical, accessible, and resonates with the target audience.

- **Commitment to Innovation**: Stay committed to innovation and the transformative potential of your educational venture.

Reflection:

Let's recall the concepts, think and write answers of the following questions to analyze your understanding of Chapter.

1. How does the iterative process of "test, iterate, enhance" contribute to the development of an effective educational product?

   _____
   _____
   _____
   _____
   _____

2. In what ways can storytelling be integrated with evidence-based results to create compelling educational content?

   _____
   _____
   _____
   _____
   _____

Just think about a time when you had to use feedback to refine a project or product.

1. How did you incorporate the feedback, and what was the outcome?

   Discuss a strategy you would use to personalize learning experiences for a diverse group of learners with different needs and learning styles.

   _____
   _____
   _____
   _____
   _____

2. How can real-world applications and hands-on projects enhance the relevance and effectiveness of educational content?

   _____
   _____
   _____
   _____
   _____

3. What steps would you take to ensure that your educational product remains relevant and impactful in a rapidly changing educational landscape?

_____

_____

_____

_____

_____

Multiple Choice:

1. **What is the primary purpose of creating a Minimum Viable Product (MVP)?**

   A) To develop a feature-rich product

   B) To test assumptions and gather early feedback

   C) To avoid collecting user feedback

   D) To complete the final version of the product

2. **Which of the following is essential for ensuring educational efficacy?**

   A) Creating content that is only engaging

   B) Ignoring educational standards

   C) Constructing a learning pathway with deliberate scaffolding

   D) Avoiding real-world applications

3. **True or False:**

   Lean edupreneurship involves creating a fully developed product before testing it with users.

   A) True

   B) False

   Personalization in educational content means creating a one-size-fits-all approach for all learners.

   A) True

   B) False

Chapter 4:
Branding, Marketing, and Community Building

Building an Educational Brand

Importance of Brand Identity: Reflecting core mission and values, standing out in the educational landscape.

Crafting a Unique Selling Proposition (USP): Highlighting what makes your venture distinct and valuable.

Visual Identity: Logo, color palette, and typography that align with your brand message.

Compelling Brand Narrative: Sharing your journey, challenges, successes, and the transformative power of education.

Living Your Brand: Authenticity in interactions, content, and dedication to educational goals.

Key Concepts of Marketing with Authenticity

- **Focus on Value Creation:** Demonstrating genuine commitment to learner growth and transformation.
- **Trustworthy Marketing**: Clear and truthful messaging that reflects the core benefits of your offerings.
- **Storytelling:** Weaving together your passion for education, product's impact, and success stories.

- **Transparent Communication**: Acknowledging the iterative nature of educational innovations.
- **Encouraging Dialogue and Feedback:** Demonstrating a commitment to continuous improvement.

Key Concepts of Community Engagement and Social Responsibility

- **Engaging in Transformative Dialogues**: Listening, learning, and addressing local concerns and ambitions.
- **Fostering Partnerships**: Collaborating with local businesses, non-profits, and civic groups for community well-being.
- **Embracing Social Responsibility**: Addressing educational gaps, environmental consciousness, advocating for equity and inclusion.
- **Sustainable Educational Offerings**: Promoting global citizenship among learners.
- **Building Trust and Respect:** Volunteer initiatives, scholarship programs, and participatory workshops.

Key Points of Effective Use of Social Media and Networking

- **Building Relationships and Establishing Thought Leadership:** Creating communities that resonate with your brand's ethos.
- **Identifying Your Audience's Preferred Platforms:** Tailoring your content and presence to the right social media channels.
- **Content as Lesson Plans**: Providing valuable and informative content at every touchpoint.

- **Engaging with Your Followers**: Responding to comments, addressing concerns, and celebrating successes.

- **Networking for Collaboration**: Building meaningful relationships with educators, influencers, and potential partners.

- **Consistency in Messaging and Posting**: Maintaining a regular posting schedule to keep your audience engaged.

- **Metrics and Data-Driven Decisions**: Using analytics tools to understand content performance and refine your strategy.

- **Authenticity and Storytelling:** Letting your unique personality and passion for education shine through.

- **Encouraging User-Generated Content:** Fostering a sense of community by having followers share their stories.

- **Strategic Use of Hashtags**: Improving visibility and connecting with relevant discussions.

- **Collaborations with Influencers**: Partnering with notable figures to reach new audiences.

- **Live Sessions and Webinars**: Providing real-time engagement and deepening audience connection.

- **Targeted Paid Advertising:** Investing in paid campaigns to effectively boost reach and impact.

- **Clear Calls to Action:** Guiding followers towards taking the next step with your brand.

Reflection

Establishing Your Educational Brand

Scenario: You are the founder of "InspireEd," an online learning platform designed to provide innovative courses for lifelong learners. Your mission is to make high-quality education accessible to everyone, regardless of their background. You have just completed the initial product development phase and are now focusing on building a strong brand identity.

Define Your Brand Identity:

Activity: Write down the mission and core values of InspireEd. Describe what sets your platform apart from others in the market.

Craft Your Unique Selling Proposition (USP):

Activity: List the unique features and benefits of InspireEd's courses. Develop a concise statement that communicates your USP.

_____
_____
_____
_____
_____

Create a Visual Identity:

Activity: Design a draft of InspireEd's logo, choose a color palette, and select typography that aligns with your brand message. Explain how these elements reflect your brand's identity.

_____

_____

_____

_____

_____

Develop Your Brand Narrative:

Activity: Write a brief history of InspireEd, highlighting key milestones and challenges. Share a personal story that illustrates the transformative impact of your platform.

_____

_____

_____

_____

_____

_____

Living Your Brand:

Activity: List three ways you can show authenticity in your interactions and content. Reflect on how maintaining authenticity can build trust and loyalty among your audience.

_____
_____
_____
_____
_____

Reflection:

1. Consider your own educational goals and interests. If you were to become an edupreneur, what unique value proposition could you offer learners?

_____
_____
_____
_____
_____

2. Think about the challenges of balancing authenticity with marketing. How can you ensure your marketing efforts are genuine and resonate with your target audience?

_____
_____

3. Imagine you are launching a new educational product or service. Describe how you would leverage social media to build a community around your brand.

Bonus:

Think of an example of an educational brand that you admire. What aspects of their branding and community engagement do you find particularly effective?

Chapter 5:
Technology Integration and Crafting Learning Experiences

- **Purposeful Use of Tools**: Selecting the right technological tools is crucial. They should complement educational objectives and not be used just for their novelty.

- **Cutting-edge Technology**: Embracing the latest technology enhances learning experiences and extends the reach and efficacy of educational products.

- **Digital Fluency:** Edupreneurs must be adept with various digital tools, such as content creation platforms, learning management systems, and analytics software.

- **Content Delivery**: Effective content delivery relies on intuitive and collaborative platforms, which encourage engagement and foster a community of learners.

- **Global Classroom**: Tools like video conferencing, online forums, and virtual whiteboards enable global connectivity and interaction.

- **Data-Driven Decisions**: Analytics and data-tracking tools guide educational decisions and strategies, allowing for personalized and adaptive learning pathways.

- **Marketing Tools**: Social media and online advertising platforms amplify the brand's voice and connect with the community.

- **SEO and Content:** Crafting engaging and educational content, while leveraging SEO, helps the brand stand out in a crowded digital landscape.

- **AI and Machine Learning**: These technologies promise personalized and scalable learning experiences by offering real-time, data-driven support.

- **Transformational Learning:** Learning experiences should be more than informational; they should be transformational, igniting intellectual curiosity and fostering lifelong learning.

- **Active Learning**: Engage learners through interactive storytelling, problem-based learning, and experiential activities that encourage active participation.

- **Real-World Relevance**: Use case studies, simulations, and discussions to connect learning to real-world scenarios.

- **Accessibility and Inclusivity**: Design learning experiences that cater to diverse learning styles and needs using various formats like videos, texts, and interactive modules.

- **Continuous Assessment and Feedback**: Integrate constructive and continuous assessments to foster improvement and celebrate growth.

- **Personalized Learning:** AI and machine learning create personalized learning journeys, adapting to individual learning styles, pace, and preferences.

- **Administrative Efficiency**: AI can automate administrative tasks, allowing educators to focus on teaching and mentoring.

- **Predictive Analytics**: Machine learning analyzes data to draw insights into learning patterns, helping tailor educational content.

- **Proactive Educational Strategies:** AI-driven analytics inform strategic decisions, ensuring educational offerings remain relevant and effective.

- **Democratizing Education**: These technologies help break down barriers to education, ensuring accessibility and inclusivity, and democratizing learning globally.

- **Transformative Potential**: AI and machine learning are not just about optimizing current practices but also about innovating new approaches to learning.

- **Lifelong Learning**: These technologies foster lifelong learning and insatiable curiosity, creating dynamic and evolving educational environments.

- **Future-Oriented Education:** By integrating AI and machine learning, edupreneurs help shape a future where personalized education is the norm and every learner's potential can be fully realized.

Reflection Questions

Personal Reflection:

How do you currently use technology in your educational practices, and what changes could you make to enhance engagement and understanding for your learners?

_____

_____

_____

_____

_____

Analytical Reflection:

Reflect on a recent learning experience you designed or participated in. How did the integration (or lack) of technology impact the learning outcomes? What would you do differently next time?

_____

_____

_____

_____

_____

Future Planning:

Considering the advancements in AI and machine learning, how do you envision incorporating these technologies into your educational offerings in the next five years?

_____

_____

_____

_____

_____

Critical Reflection:

Discuss a situation where the use of a particular technological tool either significantly enhanced or hindered the learning experience. What were the key factors that led to this outcome?

_____

_____

_____

_____

_____

Inclusive Practices:

Reflect on the diversity of learning styles and needs among your learners. How can you better integrate technology to ensure that your educational experiences are accessible and inclusive for all?

_____

_____

Strategic Reflection:

How can you leverage data analytics and feedback to continuously improve your educational products and services? Provide specific examples based on your current or planned practices.

Emotional Resonance:

Think about a time when an educational experience evoked a strong emotional response in you or your learners. How did this emotion affect the learning process, and how can you design future experiences to foster positive emotional connections?

Edupreneurial Vision:

As an edupreneur, what is your vision for the future of education, and how does technology play a role in achieving this vision? What steps are you taking to realize this vision?

_____
_____
_____
_____
_____

Chapter 6:
The Business and Economics of Edupreneurship

- **Edupreneurship marries educational passion with economic precision** to create impactful ventures.
- **Understanding and applying economic principles** allows edupreneurs to navigate the balance between educational quality and financial sustainability.
- **Monetization strategies and financial planning** are essential for transforming educational innovation into viable business models.
- **Securing funding and financial oversight** are crucial for scaling and sustaining edupreneurial initiatives.
- **Premium content, freemium models, transactional models, and consulting/licensing** as key strategies.
- **Detailed financial oversight** supports growth and scalability.
- **Balancing free and paid content** to attract and retain customers.
- Managing **cash flow, investments, and return on investment (ROI)**.
- **Ensuring scalability** without compromising educational quality.

- **Creating comprehensive budgets and strategic financial plans**.
- Exploring diverse funding options and maintaining transparency with investors.
- **Financial vigilance** is crucial for long-term sustainability and growth.

Reflection

Consider you have just launched "Green Future Academy," an edupreneurial venture dedicated to providing courses on sustainable living and environmental stewardship. The academy offers a mix of free and premium content, including online courses, workshops, and certification programs. Despite initial enthusiasm, you face several challenges, including low student engagement, financial sustainability, and scaling the business.

Your feedback indicates that while the content is valuable, students find it difficult to stay engaged and interactive with the material.

1. How could you integrate technology to enhance student engagement and interactivity in your courses?

_____
_____
_____
_____

2. What specific digital tools or platforms could you use to create a more cohesive and immersive learning experience?

_____
_____
_____
_____
_____

3. How can you balance the use of technology with pedagogical principles to ensure the learning experience remains meaningful and impactful?

_____
_____
_____
_____
_____

Some students struggle to keep up with the pace and content of the courses, indicating a need for more personalized learning paths.

1. What role could AI and machine learning play in creating more personalized learning paths for your students?

   _____
   _____
   _____
   _____
   _____

2. How would you ensure that the adaptive learning technology you implement effectively addresses the diverse learning styles and needs of your students?

   _____
   _____
   _____
   _____
   _____

As your academy grows, you face financial challenges in scaling up operations, such as hiring additional staff and investing in advanced technology.

1. How would you approach creating a detailed financial plan to manage the growth of your venture?

   _____
   _____
   _____
   _____
   _____

2. How can you maintain the quality and integrity of your educational offerings while managing the financial aspects of scaling up?

   _____
   _____
   _____
   _____
   _____

You are passionate about making your courses accessible and affordable to underprivileged communities, but struggle to find a business model that is both impactful and economically viable.

1. What innovative business models can you explore to balance accessibility and financial sustainability?

   _____
   _____
   _____
   _____

2. How can you measure and communicate the social impact of your educational offerings to attract socially conscious investors or donors?

   _____
   _____
   _____
   _____

3. What partnerships or collaborations could you pursue to enhance your educational mission while ensuring economic viability?

   _____
   _____
   _____
   _____

Chapter 7:
Leadership, Team Building, and Operational Excellence

Leadership and Team Building in Edupreneurship

Visionary Leadership:

- Edupreneurial leadership harmonizes vision with actionable strategy.
- Inspires others to believe in and contribute to a shared educational mission.
- Fosters an entrepreneurial spirit within team members, encouraging innovation.

Constructing a Cohesive Team:

- Diverse skills and backgrounds create a resilient and innovative team.
- A collaborative environment enhances creativity and open communication.
- Recognizing each team member's value is crucial for growth and adaptability.

Operational Excellence:

- Requires meticulous processes, continuous improvement, and value delivery.
- Involves a balance of systems and processes to maintain sustained productivity.
- Emphasizes adaptability and efficiency to navigate market and educational changes.

Operational Excellence

- Lean Processes and Continuous Improvement:
- Clear procedures and protocols are essential.
- Emphasizes the importance of ongoing refinement and evolution of best practices.
- Automation and delegation free up human capital for strategic objectives.

Responsiveness and Agility:

- Adapting to educational needs and market trends is vital.
- Agile methodologies allow for purposeful pivots and adjustments.
- Continuous feedback from learners and educators informs necessary changes.

Commitment to Quality:

- Ensuring high standards in every educational interaction.
- Building trust and confidence through consistent value delivery.

- Aiming for long-term contributions and impactful changes in education.

Hiring, Managing Teams, and Fostering Innovation

Strategic Hiring:

- Selecting individuals who align with the mission and bring diverse skills.
- Balancing educators and tech experts to translate ideas into tangible products.

Empowering Leadership:

- Adopting a collaborative and empowering leadership style.
- Encouraging active listening, emotional intelligence, and open feedback.
- Maintaining flexibility to adapt to the rapidly evolving educational landscape.

Culture of Innovation:

- Promoting out-of-the-box thinking and viewing failure as a learning step.
- Celebrating creative risk-taking and cross-disciplinary collaboration.
- Providing continuous professional development and staying abreast of industry trends.

Team Development:

- Offering opportunities for workshops, conferences, and industry events.
- Developing a shared vision and clear communication channels.
- Creating a culture of trust, enthusiasm, and mutual respect.

Reflection:

Reflect on Your Vision: Write down your vision for your edupreneurial venture. Consider what you aim to achieve in the educational sector.

Vision Statement: _____

Actionable Strategy: Break down your vision into three actionable strategies.

Strategy 1: _____

Strategy 2: _____

Strategy 3: _____

Encouraging Innovation: How can you create an environment that fosters creativity and innovation? Provide specific examples.

1._____
_____

2._____
_____

3._____
_____

Creating a Collaborative Environment: List three strategies to promote open communication and collaboration within your team.

1._____
_____

2._____
_____

3._____
_____

Defining Procedures: Outline the key procedures and protocols essential for your venture's operations.

1._____
_____

2._____
_____

3._____
_____

Leveraging Technology

Automation Opportunities: Identify tasks that can be automated to improve efficiency.

_____

_____

_____

Delegation Plan: Create a delegation plan that empowers team members and promotes ownership.

Task 1:
_____

Responsible Team Member: _____

Task 2:
_____

Responsible Team Member: _____

Market Responsiveness

Staying Informed: List the sources you will use to stay updated on market trends and educational needs.

_____

_____

_____

4. **Agile Adjustments**: Describe how you will implement agile methodologies to adapt to market changes.

_____
_____
_____

Feedback Loops

Creating Feedback Loops: Design a feedback loop system to gather insights from learners and educators.

_____
_____
_____

Using Feedback for Improvement: How will you utilize this feedback to refine your educational offerings?

_____
_____
_____

Leadership Reflection

Self-Assessment: Reflect on your leadership style. What are your strengths and areas for improvement?

Strengths: _____

Areas for Improvement: _____

Goal Setting: Set two specific goals to improve your leadership skills over the next six months.

Goal 1: _____

Goal 2: _____

Team Dynamics

Assessing Team Dynamics: Reflect on your team's dynamics. What is working well, and what could be improved?

Strengths: _____

Areas for Improvement: _____

Building Stronger Bonds: Plan two activities or strategies to strengthen your team's cohesion and morale.

Activity/Strategy 1:

_____

_____

_____

Activity/Strategy 2:

_____

_____

_____

Chapter 8: Navigating Legalities and Ethics

1. Importance of Legal and Ethical Understanding

Legal and Ethical Compass: Edupreneurship requires a profound understanding of legal and ethical landscapes to ensure both the protection and integrity of educational ventures.

Trust and Reputation: Upholding high standards in legal and ethical practices builds trust and cements the reputation of an educational enterprise.

2. Legal and Ethical Foundations

Compliance and Integrity: Understanding laws related to educational content (e.g., copyright, licensing) and maintaining a robust code of ethics are fundamental.

Data Privacy: Adhering to regulations like FERPA and developing transparent privacy policies is crucial for protecting sensitive student information.

Intellectual Property (IP): Protecting original content and using third-party materials responsibly ensures that creativity is safeguarded and respected.

3. Protecting Intellectual Property

Types of IP Protection: Copyrights protect curricula and written works, trademarks safeguard brand features, and patents may apply to new educational tools.

Defensive and Offensive IP Strategy: Protecting your work from unauthorized use and carving out market space through proper IP management.

Balance Between Sharing and Commercialization: Licensing agreements can help share educational materials while maintaining rights and revenue streams.

4. Privacy and Ethics in Education

Championing Privacy: Beyond compliance, building trust through transparent practices and safeguarding student data.

Ethical Considerations: Avoiding conflicts of interest, ensuring accessibility, and upholding academic integrity are crucial for ethical edupreneurship.

Respect for IP: Honoring the intellectual property rights of others fosters a culture of respect and collaboration.

5. Collaborations and Partnerships

Strategic Partnerships: Building alliances that align with your vision and values, offering mutual benefits, and enhancing educational impact.

Clear Agreements: Defining contributions, responsibilities, and benefits to prevent discord and ensure transparency.

Nurturing Relationships: Regular communication, joint milestones, and continuous feedback help partnerships evolve and remain effective.

Assessment and Reflection: Tracking progress and outcomes to inform future collaborations and enhance overall educational impact.

Reflection

Consider a situation where you have developed an innovative educational tool. Reflect on the steps you would take to ensure that your tool complies with copyright and licensing laws. How would you integrate a robust code of ethics into your venture's operations?

Key Points to Consider:

- The importance of seeking legal advice to understand copyright and licensing requirements.
- The development of a code of ethics that guides daily decision-making and interactions.
- Ensuring transparency in communications with stakeholders and learners.

_____
_____
_____
_____
_____
_____
_____

Protecting Intellectual Property

Imagine you have created a comprehensive online course. Reflect on the strategies you would use to protect your intellectual property. How would you balance the need to protect your work with the desire to share knowledge?

Key Points to Consider:

- The different types of IP protection available (copyright, trademark, patent).
- The importance of maintaining detailed records of the creation process.
- Strategies for licensing agreements that allow others to use your materials while protecting your rights.

Ethical Decision-Making in Edupreneurship

Reflect on a time when you faced an ethical dilemma in a professional setting. How did you approach the situation, and what did you learn from it? How can these lessons be applied to your future edupreneurial endeavors?

Key Points to Consider:

- The process of evaluating the ethical implications of your decisions.
- The importance of empathy and transparency in resolving ethical dilemmas.
- Applying lessons learned to create a more ethical and trustworthy venture.

_____
_____
_____
_____
_____
_____
_____
_____
_____
_____
_____
_____

Chapter 9:
Measuring Impact and Scaling Your Venture

Measuring Success and Impact

- Holistic Metrics: Success is measured not only by financial gains but by educational outcomes, learner engagement, and community impact.

- Quantitative Measures: Standardized test scores, course completion rates, and real-world application of learned skills.

- Qualitative Measures: Personal success stories, peer recognition, and community testimonials.

- Continuous Improvement: Establishing a feedback loop through surveys, focus groups, and data analytics to refine and enhance offerings.

- Long-Term Impact: Focusing on sustainable, transformative effects on the educational landscape.

Scaling Strategies for Edupreneurs

- Diversification: Expanding educational products or services to meet emerging needs and market trends.

- Operational Efficiency: Streamlining processes through automation and delegation, ensuring quality management as demand increases.

- Team Building: Hiring and nurturing a team that shares the vision and can adapt to changes.
- Strategic Partnerships: Forming alliances with complementary organizations to combine resources, expertise, and networks.
- Digital Presence: Leveraging online platforms and digital marketing to reach a global audience while maintaining quality and personalization.

Going Global: Crossing Borders and Cultures

- Cultural Sensitivity: Adapting educational content to meet the diverse needs and preferences of global learners.
- Transcreation: Beyond translation, ensuring the motivational and educational essence of content is preserved in different languages.
- Local Collaboration: Partnering with local experts to ensure authenticity and cultural relevance.
- Building Trust: Immersing in local educational communities, understanding regulatory requirements, and networking with local influencers.
- Technological Integration: Using technology to facilitate seamless delivery and integration of educational content across borders.

Reflection:

1. What are the primary quantitative metrics you currently use to measure your venture's success?

   _____
   _____
   _____
   _____

2. What new educational products or services could you introduce to diversify your offerings?

   _____
   _____
   _____
   _____

3. What steps will you take to diversify your app's offerings?

   _____
   _____
   _____
   _____

4. What cultural differences might you need to consider when adapting your educational content for a global audience?

_____
_____
_____
_____
_____

5. What steps can you take to ensure that your impact is sustainable and long-term?

_____
_____
_____
_____
_____

Scenario: You have developed an online course that has been well-received by a small group of beta testers. You are preparing to launch the course on a larger scale and need to determine how to measure its success effectively.

Questions:

1. Which quantitative metrics will you use to evaluate the success of your online course?

   _____
   _____
   _____
   _____

2. How will you collect qualitative feedback from your learners to complement your quantitative data?

   _____
   _____
   _____
   _____

3. What methods will you employ to ensure continuous improvement of the course based on learner feedback?

_____
_____
_____
_____
_____

Scenario: You plan to launch your educational program in a new country. This requires adapting your content to fit the local culture and educational system while maintaining its core values.

Questions:

1. How will you adapt your content to meet the cultural preferences of the new market?

   _____
   _____
   _____
   _____
   _____

2. What strategies will you use to ensure the quality and effectiveness of translations?

   _____
   _____
   _____
   _____
   _____

3. Identify local experts or organizations you can partner with to enhance your program's relevance.

_____
_____
_____
_____
_____

Chapter 10:
The Future of Edupreneurship and Personal Growth

- The future of education is a fusion of entrepreneurship and pedagogy, creating a vibrant space for innovation and societal learning.

- Edupreneurs: They are individuals who combine educational expertise with business acumen to address educational gaps and create new learning experiences.

- Successful educational ventures prioritize the needs of learners, crafting solutions that target specific problems and embrace flexible learning pathways.

- Technological Integration: Technology plays a vital role in edupreneurship, enabling educators to create engaging online platforms, personalize learning experiences, and leverage data for continuous improvement.

- Community Building: Fostering a strong community around your venture is essential. This can involve collaborative networks, forums for knowledge exchange, and user-generated content.

- Identifying a need in the educational landscape

- Developing innovative solutions that address this need

- Building a strong brand that resonates with your target audience
- Utilizing technology effectively to create engaging and personalized learning experiences
- Fostering a community around your venture to build trust and social impact
- Balancing creativity with sound business practices to ensure the sustainability of your venture
- Continuous learning and personal growth to stay ahead of the curve in the ever-evolving educational landscape.

Reflection:

1. Consider your own interests and skills. What educational niche could you potentially fill as an edupreneur?

   _____
   _____
   _____
   _____

2. Think about the challenges of balancing creativity with financial viability. How can you ensure your educational venture is both innovative and sustainable?

   _____
   _____
   _____
   _____

3. Research an edupreneur or educational company that you admire. What aspects of their approach to branding and community engagement do you find particularly effective? Explain your answer.

   _____
   _____
   _____
   _____
   _____

Design a mock advertisement for your educational product or service using the principles of authentic marketing discussed in the chapter.

_____
_____
_____
_____
_____
_____
_____
_____
_____
_____
_____
_____
_____
_____
_____
_____
_____
_____
_____
_____

Case Scenario

Maya is a seasoned yoga instructor with a deep passion for mindfulness and wellness. Witnessing the growing demand for stress-reduction techniques, she decides to launch her own online yoga platform, "Flow with Maya." Maya meticulously crafts a series of beginner-friendly yoga routines, meditation exercises, and breathing techniques, all accessible with a monthly subscription.

Initial Success: Leveraging her existing network and social media presence, Maya attracts a dedicated following within the first few months. Students appreciate her approachable teaching style and the convenience of practicing yoga at home.

The Challenges Mount: While initial growth is promising, Maya soon finds herself overwhelmed with managing all aspects of her business. Creating high-quality content, marketing "Flow with Maya," providing customer support, and handling administrative tasks become a daily juggle. The workload cuts into her time for personal practice and creativity, diminishing the joy she once found in teaching yoga.

Reflection Points:

- **Strengths and Weaknesses**: Identify Maya's strengths as an edupreneur (e.g., passion, teaching expertise). What are her weaknesses that are hindering her growth (e.g., lack of business experience, limited resources)?

_____

_____

_____

_____

- **Sustainability and Scalability:** How can Maya build a more sustainable and scalable business model for "Flow with Maya"? Consider potential solutions like outsourcing tasks, building partnerships, or creating tiered subscription plans.

_____
_____
_____
_____

- **Work-Life Balance:** Discuss the importance of maintaining a healthy work-life balance for edupreneurs like Maya. How can she prioritize her well-being while managing the demands of her business?

_____
_____
_____
_____

- **Community Building:** What strategies could Maya employ to foster a stronger community around "Flow with Maya"? This could involve online forums, student challenges, or live Q&A sessions.

_____
_____
_____
_____

Imagine you are a mentor advising Maya. What specific recommendations would you offer to help her overcome these challenges and thrive as an edupreneur?

Appendix A:
Resources for Edupreneurs

As we explore edupreneurship, it's clear that available resources can propel an aspiring edupreneur from concept to reality. Transformative ideas don't exist in a vacuum; they thrive with the support of a rich ecosystem. Here, you'll find a treasure trove of resources, from communities that spark innovation to tools that forge the path ahead.

Online Communities and Networks

Seeking wisdom from a crowd of like-minded visionaries can light the way for your edupreneurial venture. Participate in online forums, LinkedIn groups, the Edupreneurs Network, or Facebook communities specifically for edupreneurs to exchange ideas, seek advice, and find mentorship. There are multiple websites that provide comprehensive information on edupreneurship. There are podcasts and webinars bursting with insights on the edupreneurial process. They offer interviews with industry leaders, discussions on the latest trends, and strategies for business growth. Here are a few to consider:

- The Empowered Edupreneur: Michelle Smit coaches edupreneurs on building an online business
- The Dr. Will Show: Stories from the frontline of edupreneurship

- Teacherpreneurs: Tina Deboree discusses a range of topics on teacherpreneurship

- Legends Lab: Where experts become stand-out legends in edupreneurship

- Designing Schools: Dr. Sabba Quidwai discusses how empathy cultures lead to cultures of innovation

- My First Million: Sam Parr and Shaan Puri brainstorm new business ideas based on trends and opportunities

- The Side Hustle: Nick Loper discusses entrepreneurship topics you can actually apply

- Entrepreneurs On Fire: John Lee Dumas focuses on sharing a roadmap to financial freedom and fulfillment

- How I Built This: Guy Raz interviews the world's best-known entrepreneurs to learn how they built their iconic brands.

Conferences and Workshops

Nothing matches the electric energy of being in a room full of entrepreneurs and creatives. Conferences and workshops fuel innovation and foster connections. Keep an eye on:

- South by Southwest EDU (SXSW EDU): Annual conference with various educational innovation tracks.

- ASU GSV Summit: A national conference that brings together leaders in education and business to discuss the future of teaching and learning.

- EdTechX Global Conference & Expo: An international meeting place for the edtech community.

- Edupreneur Summit: Conference designed to help edupreneurs succeed in online education.

- Eduventures Summit: Edupreneur summit focusing on higher education

Educational Blogs and News Sites

To stay ahead, keep abreast of the latest happenings in the educational and entrepreneurial sectors. Here's where to turn for news and thought leadership:

- EdWeek Market Brief: The latest news on the business of education
- EdTech Magazine: It focuses on higher education and K-12 uses of technology
- The Hechinger Report: Independent journalism on innovation and inequality in education
- ASCD: Education and Leadership Journal
- schoolceo: A journal that focuses on school district solutions

As you navigate the edupreneur's landscape, remember that the path is not linear. It's a journey of continual learning, adapting, and growing. The resources listed here are just the beginning. They can help turn the wheels of progress and innovation, opening doors to new possibilities in the realm of education. Arm yourself with knowledge, reach out to connect, and let your vision for transformative educational experiences take flight.

Tools for Edupreneurs

Don't reinvent the wheel when there are tools at your disposal designed to refine and enhance your educational offerings. Harness the power of these platforms:

- Canva for Education: Create visually compelling educational materials with ease
- Google for Education: Tools that foster collaboration and innovation in the classroom and beyond
- Kickstarter: Crowdfunding platform where you can gauge interest and secure funding for educational projects
- ChatGPT: an online tool that can support your edupreneurial venture in various ways, including enhancing your educational offerings, streamlining operations, and improving customer engagement
- Gemini: a similar platform to ChatGPT that can support your venture

Appendix B:
Glossary of Edupreneurship Terms

As we embrace the journey of transforming education through the lens of edupreneurship, mastering the vocabulary of this evolving field is crucial. The following glossary is a compass to navigate the rich landscape of concepts, strategies, and tools that are part and parcel of edupreneurship.

A

Adaptive Learning: An educational approach that adjusts to each student's individual needs and learning styles.

Agile Learning: A flexible and iterative approach to education that emphasizes rapid prototyping, continuous improvement, and feedback.

Artificial Intelligence (AI): The ability of machines to simulate human intelligence processes, including learning and problem solving. AI has the potential to personalize learning, automate tasks, and provide valuable insights in education.

B

Blended Learning: A hybrid approach combining traditional classroom instruction with online learning elements.

C

Competency-Based Education: A system of education that measures student progress based on demonstrating specific skills or competencies rather than on seat time or credit hours.

Consultant: An individual or firm that provides expert advice and guidance to businesses and organizations in specific areas, such as edupreneurship.

D

Design Thinking: A problem-solving approach that involves empathy, ideation, and experimentation to create innovative solutions.

E

E-Learning (Online Learning): The use of digital technologies, such as computers and the internet, to deliver and enhance learning experiences.

Edupreneur: A term used to describe an individual who combines education and entrepreneurship to create, develop, and sell innovative educational products or services.

Educational Entrepreneurship: The process of creating and leading innovation in the field of education, often involving the development of new educational products, services, or approaches.

Educational Leadership: The ability to provide direction, guidance, and support within an educational institution to improve teaching and learning.

F

Flipped Classroom: A teaching approach that involves learners reviewing material at home and then applying what they have learned in class through discussions, projects, and other interactive activities.

G

Gamification: The use of game elements, such as points, badges, and leaderboards, in non-game contexts, such as education.

I

Intellectual Property (IP): Creations of the mind, such as inventions, literary and artistic works, designs, and symbols, which can be owned and protected by law. For edupreneurs, this could include educational resources, software, and course materials.

L

Learning Analytics: The measurement, collection, analysis, and reporting of data about learners and their contexts, for purposes of understanding and optimizing learning and the environments in which it occurs.

Learning Management System (LMS): A software application used to plan, implement, and assess a specific learning process.

M

Microlearning: A learning approach that involves the delivery of educational content in small, manageable chunks.

MOOC (Massive Open Online Course): A free online course that is open to an unlimited number of participants.

O

Open Educational Practices (OEP): The use of open technologies, open resources, and open practices to support learning.

Open Educational Resources (OER): Teaching, learning, and research materials in any medium that reside in the public domain or have been released under an open license that permits their free use and repurposing by others.

P

Personalized Learning: A student-centered approach to education that tailors instruction, content, pace, and assessments to meet the individual needs, skills, and interests of each learner.

R

Revenue: The income generated from the sale of goods or services. In edupreneurship, revenue can come from subscriptions, course fees, product sales, or other means.

S

Scalability: The ability of a business to grow and increase its output without significant additional resources.

Social Learning: A learning approach that emphasizes the role of social interactions, conversations, and experiences in the learning process.

Strategic Planning: The process of defining an organization's goals, developing strategies to achieve them, and allocating resources to implement those strategies.

V

Venture: A risky or daring business undertaking. In edupreneurship, this could refer to developing and launching a new educational product or service.

Appendix C:
Checklists and Templates for Start-Up Success

I. Self-Assessment:

Strengths and Weaknesses Identify strengths in educational expertise, entrepreneurial skills, leadership abilities, and financial management or marketing weaknesses.

Passions and Interests Reflect on personal interests within the education sector, whether it's early childhood education, technology integration, or professional development.

Unique Skills and Experiences List any specialized skills or experiences that set you apart, such as teaching experience, curriculum development, or educational technology proficiency.

Short-term and Long-term Goals Establish specific, measurable goals for the short-term (1-2 years) and long-term (3-5 years), including objectives related to revenue, market penetration, and impact on education.

II. Market Research:

Target Audience Define your target audience, which may include teachers, parents, schools, specific age groups, demographics, or geographical areas.

Needs and Pain Points Conduct surveys, interviews, or market research to identify your target audience's primary needs, challenges, and pain points.

Competitors and Unique Value Proposition Analyze competitors in the market, identify gaps, and determine the unique value proposition that sets you apart from existing offerings.

Market Size and Growth Potential Research the size and growth potential of the education market, considering factors like demographic trends, technological advancements, and regulatory changes.

III. Product/Service Development:

Offering Description Define the product or service you will offer, detailing its features, benefits, and how it addresses the needs of your target audience.

Alignment with Audience Needs Ensure your offering directly addresses your target audience's identified pain points and preferences.

Unique Selling Proposition (USP) Articulate your USP clearly, highlighting what makes your offering distinct and superior to competitors.

Pricing, Promotion, and Distribution Develop pricing strategies, promotional tactics, and distribution channels that align with your target audience and market positioning.

IV. Financial Planning:

Startup and Ongoing Costs Estimate all startup expenses and ongoing operational costs, including overhead, marketing, technology, and personnel.

Revenue Streams and Pricing Strategy Identify primary revenue streams and establish a pricing strategy that maximizes profitability while remaining competitive.

Break-even Points and Profitability Projections Calculate break-even points and create financial projections to forecast revenue, expenses, and profitability over time.

Financial Resources Needed: Determine the financial resources required to launch and sustain your venture, considering sources such as personal savings, loans, investors, or grants.

V. Operational Planning:

Processes and Systems: Define operational processes and systems for product development, marketing, sales, customer service, and administrative tasks.

Technology and Tools: Select appropriate technology and tools to streamline operations, enhance productivity, and support business objectives.

Organizational Structure and Management: Design an organizational structure delineating roles, responsibilities, and reporting relationships, along with a management style fostering collaboration and innovation.

Policies and Procedures: Establish policies and procedures to ensure legal compliance, ethical conduct, and risk management across all aspects of the business.

VI. Implementation and Monitoring:

Action Steps and Timelines: Develop a detailed implementation plan with specific action steps, timelines, and responsible parties to execute the strategic objectives.

Key Performance Indicators (KPIs): Define measurable KPIs aligned with business goals to track performance and progress over time.

Continuous Improvement Strategies: Implement strategies for continuous improvement and innovation, such as gathering feedback, analyzing data, and adapting to market changes.

Contingency Planning: Identify potential challenges and setbacks and develop contingency plans to mitigate risks and ensure business continuity.

VII. Support System:

Mentors, Advisors, and Partners: Cultivate relationships with mentors, advisors, and strategic partners who can provide guidance, expertise, and support throughout your entrepreneurial journey.

Work-Life Balance and Self-Care: Prioritize strategies for maintaining work-life balance, managing stress, and prioritizing self-care to sustain long-term success.

Professional Development and Networking: Invest in ongoing professional development opportunities and networking activities to expand your knowledge, skills, and connections within the education industry.

Community Building Strategies: Build a solid and supportive community of fellow edupreneurs, educators, and stakeholders through networking events, online forums, and collaborative projects.

www.ingramcontent.com/pod-product-compliance
Lightning Source LLC
Chambersburg PA
CBHW062222080426
42734CB00010B/1997